unpacking
the gift

Anglican resources for theological
reflection on *The Gift of Authority*

edited by Peter Fisher

CHURCH HOUSE
PUBLISHING

Church House Publishing
Church House
Great Smith Street
London
SW1P 3NZ

ISBN 0 7151 5767 1

GS Misc 697

Published 2002 for the Council for
Christian Unity of the Archbishops'
Council by Church House Publishing

*Copyright © The Archbishops'
Council 2002*

Typeset in: Franklin Gothic 9.5/11

Printed by The Cromwell Press,
Trowbridge, Wiltshire

The Faith and Order Advisory Group (FOAG) is a constituent
body of the Church of England's Council for Christian Unity (CCU).
In order to stimulate discussion of *The Gift of Authority*, FOAG
decided not to attempt to produce a single agreed 'official'
response at this stage, but instead to bring together a collection
of independent essays reflecting a variety of different ways of
responding to the ARCIC text. This way of working means that
each of the essayists is responsible only for his or her own work,
and the essays should not be seen as expressing the views of
either FOAG or the Council for Christian Unity as a whole.

contents

contributors   iv

foreword   v

chapter one the context of *The Gift of Authority* in the history   1
of Anglican–Roman Catholic dialogue
Stephen Platten

chapter two authority: gift or threat?   14
Mary Tanner

chapter three 'yes'and 'no' – a response to *The Gift of Authority*   33
Martin Davie

chapter four an ecumenical hermeneutic of trust   60
Christopher Hill

chapter five *The Gift of Authority* in the Church of England:
sketching a contextual theology   76
Martyn Percy

chapter six it's the thought that counts:
reflections from local contexts in England   94
Flora Winfield

chapter seven in conclusion   100
Peter Fisher

notes   108

index   117

contributors

Dr Martin Davie	Secretary of the Faith and Order Advisory Group (FOAG), Theological Secretary of the Council for Christian Unity of the Archbishops' Council and Theological Consultant to the House of Bishops of the Church of England
The Revd Canon Peter Fisher	Principal of the Queen's Foundation for Ecumenical Theological Education, Birmingham and a member of FOAG
The Rt Revd Christopher Hill	Bishop of Stafford and Vice-Chairman of FOAG
The Revd Canon Dr Martyn Percy	Director of the Lincoln Institute, Sheffield and a member of FOAG
The Very Revd Stephen Platten	Dean of Norwich, member of FOAG and formerly Archbishop of Canterbury's Secretary for Ecumenical Affairs
Dr Mary Tanner OBE	Ecumenical author, Former General Secretary of the Council for Christian Unity and Moderator of the Faith and Order Group of the WCC
The Revd Flora Winfield	At the time of writing, Local Unity Secretary of the Council for Christian Unity; from September 2002, Canon of Winchester

foreword

One of the few things that can confidently be said to be unanimously agreed about *The Gift of Authority*, the 1999 report of the Anglican–Roman Catholic International Commission (ARCIC), is that it is controversial.

The theme of authority is of vital importance not only for Christians longing for Jesus' prayer to be answered that his disciples might all be one, but also for humankind in general asking whether saving truth is to be found and even if, in an allegedly postmodern age, the question means anything anyway.

This collection of essays aims to help readers think through some of the issues involved. All of the authors are either present or past members of the Faith and Order Advisory Group of the Church of England.

In these pages you will find a wide variety of approaches, warm appreciation for the seriousness with which the Commission has engaged with one of the most fundamental of ecumenical issues and, not surprisingly, varying degrees of enthusiasm for the thesis of the Report itself.

The recent history of Anglican–Roman Catholic theological dialogue is described and set within the wider context of the ecumenical movement. At a time when some ecumenists seem to have lost a bit of heart it is good to be reminded of some of what has been achieved in the past half-century. It is an indication of the progress that has been made that Christians are generally now able to consider their differences as within a single family.

Who would have imagined when ARCIC began its work in the 1960s that before the end of the century the Bishop of Rome would be inviting the leaders and theologians of other Churches to 'engage with me in a patient and fraternal dialogue' concerning '. . . the forms in which [his] ministry may accomplish a service of love recognized by all concerned'(Encyclical, *Ut Unum Sint*, 1995)? The House of Bishops of the Church of England (in the 1997 report *May They All Be One*) responded warmly to that invitation and identified some of the same issues as have been raised in response to *The Gift of Authority*.

As is well known, *The Gift of Authority* makes the remarkable suggestion that there might be a provisional recognition of universal primacy even in advance of the establishment of the full communion of the Church. This approach is similar to the provisions of the Ecumenical Canons already in force whereby, in view of our common commitment to the coming unity of the Church, the Church of England allows and even encourages a limited 'living of the future today'.

Nevertheless, it is clear that the way to the full visible unity of the Church (to which Anglicans, Roman Catholics and many other Christians are committed) admits of no short cuts. Too much is at stake, and it is to the credit of ARCIC that it has not shirked the difficult questions. Its method however has not been to rework old controversies, but to try to look behind them at the fundamentals of Christian faith. The Commission has thus been a faithful exponent of this increasingly shared ecumenical method.

At the same time, responses to *The Gift of Authority* have highlighted the extent to which the issue of authority remains problematic – not, of course, only between the Churches but also within them. These essays point to the way in which neither Anglicans nor Roman Catholics can feel totally happy about all aspects of the exercise of authority in their own Churches. Critical voices are raised from evangelical and contemporary cultural perspectives, as well as by those who see *The Gift of Authority* as exemplifying a widespread tendency in ecumenical dialogue to idealize the Church and not engage as seriously as necessary with concrete questions of power.

It all makes for an interesting and lively collection of essays, which we offer as a contribution to the ongoing debate about the vital and difficult matter of authority in the Church. As Chairman of FOAG, I thank most warmly all our contributors, and above all Peter Fisher who has edited the volume.

✠ John Cicestr

chapter 1

the context of *The Gift of Authority* in the history of Anglican–Roman Catholic dialogue

Stephen Platten

In December 1960, Dr Geoffrey Fisher called on Pope John XXIII on his way back from a visit to Jerusalem. It is difficult to exaggerate the significance of Fisher's visit. This was the first time that an Archbishop of Canterbury had visited the Pope since Archbishop Arundel had travelled to Rome in 1397. More to the point, of course, is the fact that this was the very first such visit since the fracturing of Western Christendom at the Reformation; it was indeed the first formal move by the Church of England to open up official channels of communication with the Holy See. There remain interesting ironies in relation to the Archbishop's meeting. To begin with, Fisher was not an obvious candidate to take such an initiative; he came from the establishment centre of the Church of England and was known, on occasion, to display suspicion about Roman Catholic triumphalism in England. Furthermore, despite the acclaimed openness of Giovanni Roncalli, who had been elected two years previously as Pope John XXIII, the Curia was less relaxed. The Secretariat of State did its best to play down the significance of the visit and to reduce publicity to a minimum. Vatican officials agreed that there should be no photographs of the Archbishop with the Pope, no press release following the visit and no meeting of the Archbishop with Cardinal Augustin Bea, who had recently been appointed as the first President of the newly constituted Vatican Secretariat for the Promotion of Unity amongst Christians.

Ultimately, most of these obstacles were swept away. Cardinal Bea was keen to meet Archbishop Fisher and he did so. In response to this, Fisher decided immediately to send a liaison representative to live in Rome to study the preparations for the Vatican Council and to be available for further consultations with the Archbishop's Office, as the Council progressed. A new era had dawned. This early background is important in understanding the context out of which *The Gift of Authority* has ultimately grown. It demonstrates only too clearly earlier patterns of authority within both Communions. It also indicates the significance of the changes wrought by Pope John not only in the Council itself, but also in the establishment of what eventually became known as the Pontifical Council for the Promotion of Christian Unity. Even this development needs to be placed against a broader cultural and ecclesiological background. The twentieth century had already seen remarkable developments with regard to Christian unity. The Edinburgh Conference of 1910, and the growth of both the *faith and order* and *life and work* movements, had led eventually to the establishment of the World Council of Churches (WCC) in 1948. Anglicans had played an important part in clearing the path which led to the establishment of the World Council, notably George Bell and Oliver Tompkins; Fisher too had been active as a President of the WCC. There had also been ground-breaking initiatives from within the Roman Catholic Church, particularly in the setting up of the Week of Prayer for Christian Unity through the inspiration of the Abbé Couturier. Then, in Britain, the 'Sword of the Spirit' movement pioneered by Cardinal Hinsley introduced to the Roman Catholic community in England seeds of a more ecumenical age.

The 1960s was, of course, a period of considerable cultural ferment in the Western world as a whole. Attitudes to authority were challenged in the political arena and, despite the persistence of the Cold War between East and West, a freer intellectual atmosphere was there to be breathed. It manifested itself in the United States of America in the excitement surrounding the election of John Kennedy as President and in his challenge to the fossilized and fossilizing authority structures of Soviet communism both during the Cuban crisis of 1962 and his posture on Berlin. Many at home in the USA also believed Kennedy heralded a new age of social justice, especially in relation to racial harmony. On the eastern side of the Atlantic too, politicians spoke of the dawning of a new age; Harold Macmillan told the people of Britain that they 'had never had it so good', and he, in turn, in the Profumo crisis had his authority tested as never before as the media flexed newly discovered muscles. Even the prospering of satirical humour through television and radio echoed a new cultural climate.

The fresh cultural air of the 1960s issued from a world redefined both by war and by an uneasy peace. Intellectually, too, the period following the Second World War had been one of ferment and real creativity. The pre-war popularity of logical positivism, with its resistance to any philosophical reflection rooted in metaphysics (both in ethics and in religion), had given way to a more mixed philosophical economy. Ludwig Wittgenstein's seminal influence helped produce a more varied landscape in the realm of linguistic philosophy. Then, too, those who followed Kierkegaard continued the development of different forms of existentialism. Some of these thinkers, including Jean-Paul Sartre, remained inimical to belief. Others, however, embraced religion: the work of Paul Tillich, Rudolf Bultmann and John Macquarrie was of particular significance. Alongside this, the rapid development of the human sciences, notably in the area of psychology, grew in parallel with and also supported these broader existential trends within a wider culture. The broad influence of these intellectual shifts presaged a burgeoning individualism mirrored in popular culture, but which also raised questions about the appropriate manner of exercising authority within society.

This willingness to revisit accepted patterns of authority was reflected on both sides of the Atlantic in new patterns of theological thinking. In Britain, this was made manifest in what became known as 'South Bank theology' epitomized in the controversy surrounding Bishop John Robinson's paperback *Honest to God*.[1] In Germany and in North America, both biblical and doctrinal theologians were similarly posing radical questions for the Churches themselves, and in response to Christian 'tradition'. The most extreme reactions could be seen amongst moralists in the exposition of 'situation ethics' and ultimately amongst doctrinal writers with the advent of the so-called 'death of God theology'. Despite the dangers normally associated with the collapse of familiar boundaries, a new freedom of thought and practice also emerged. To change the metaphor, there was effectively a dramatic climate change, which made possible the emergence of revised thinking about authority in the Christian community. This new freer atmosphere allowed for easier exchange; all the Churches began to appreciate the possibility of being able to breathe this exhilarating fresh air, which was now common to all. It was this new atmosphere that would prosper the growth of ecumenical dialogue in the formative ARCIC years.

The new climate, then, that has thus far been described, positively encouraged the growth of ecumenical endeavour and the beginnings of ecclesiological rapprochement. This was one of the most fertile periods for the work of 'councils of Churches' worldwide and for developing initiatives, which brought together people from the entire spectrum of Christian tradition. Ecumenism was in the air. Nevertheless, it was the opening of the Second Vatican Ecumenical Council in September/October 1962, which undeniably was the most crucial development in furthering the cause of Christian unity. The calling of the Council itself implied a new self-understanding within the Roman Catholic Church. The Decree on Ecumenism, *Unitatis Redintegratio*,[2] was promulgated in November 1964. In the words of this document, the Church of God 'subsisted in' rather than simply was the Catholic Church; Roman Catholics let go of what others had seen as totalitarian ecclesiological claims. This dramatic shift, combined with Pope Paul VI's knowledge and understanding of the Church of England, paved the way for the next crucial move forward in Anglican–Roman Catholic relations, the visit of Archbishop Michael Ramsey to the Pope in 1966. From this grew two crucial initiatives, which were to be essential in building the foundations for realistic theological conversations both on the path to unity as a whole and, more specifically, on the issue of authority. First of all, Archbishop Ramsey (with the support of Pope Paul VI) set up the Anglican Centre in Rome. This represented a permanent place of liaison between Lambeth and the Vatican. Secondly, in the Common Declaration at the 1966 meeting between the two leaders, formal dialogue between the Roman Catholic Church and the Anglican Communion was inaugurated. The Declaration noted that there was to be 'a serious dialogue . . . founded on the Gospels and on the ancient common traditions'.[3] The aim was to start with what the two Churches held in common rather than to reopen old controversies.

This work was taken forward in its detail by a Joint Preparatory Commission, which resulted in the so-called *Malta Report* published on 2 January 1968. The report recommended that the dialogue should focus on intercommunion, the doctrines of the Church, the ministry, and authority, including the 'Petrine primacy' and infallibility.[4] Two years later, the permanent Anglican–Roman Catholic International Commission (ARCIC I) met for the first time in January 1970 and engaged initially in dialogue on the three issues of the Eucharist, ministry and ordination. Thereafter the Commission decided to deal with these issues one by one. The real work of ecclesiological dialogue between the two Communions had now begun.

Ultimately, the work of ARCIC has been seminal, inasmuch as it has helped to lay the foundations for other theological dialogues between different Churches, both multilaterally and bilaterally. Part of the reason for this wider influence of ARCIC was the establishment of a unique methodology. Indeed, methodology was the first crucial issue; the ARCIC dialogue sought to reach back beyond the controversies of the sixteenth century to rediscover the common roots of our divergent traditions in Scripture and in the subsequent teaching of the Church. This methodology spawned a new matrix for theological dialogue centring on the concept of *communion* or *koinonia*. This matrix has now become an essential part of the ecumenical theological landscape, and the concept of koinonia has become the keystone of contemporary ecclesiological scholarship. This root-concept had been used and developed within the Second Vatican Council by Henri de Lubac and Yves Congar amongst others. Jean-Marie Tillard, a disciple of Congar, remained a key member of both ARCIC I and ARCIC II throughout the work of the Commission, and until his death on 13 November 2000. Tillard's seminal influence remained essential to the structure and argument of *The Gift of Authority*.

The first statement of ARCIC I was the Windsor Statement on the *Eucharist* published in 1971. This was followed by the 1973 statement on *Ministry* and *Ordination*. In the case of the statement on the Eucharist, the Commission claimed substantial agreement;[5] on ministry and ordination the Commission claimed 'that in what we have said here both Anglicans and Roman Catholics will recognise their own faith'.[6] Then, four years later, in 1977, the Commission published its first statement on authority. The Commission invited the appropriate bodies in both Communions to consider whether its 'statements expressed a unity at the level of faith sufficient to call for "closer sharing . . . in life, worship and mission"'.[7] There was a provisional response to this in the Common Declaration which issued from the meeting of Pope Paul VI with Archbishop Donald Coggan. This declaration was encouraging, and the Commission, responding to comments and criticisms, produced an *Elucidation* on authority in 1981. Section VI, Problems and Prospects, in the first statement on authority affirmed that the Commission had reached 'a consensus on authority in the Church and, in particular, on the basic principles of primacy', which they considered to be of 'fundamental importance'.[8] This was the starting point for the second statement on authority (*Authority II*) published coterminously with the *Elucidation* in 1981. The Commission did not argue that, on the matter of authority, complete or substantial agreement had been reached. Indeed, the final paragraph of *Authority II* notes: 'This does not mean that all differences have been eliminated . . . We suggest that some difficulties will not be wholly resolved until a practical initiative has been taken and our two Churches have lived together more visibly in one *koinonia*.'[9] In other words, the Commission realized that there was further work to be done on authority and it proposed ways of achieving this. Just such a proposal (in a modest way) is made in *The Gift of Authority*, particularly in suggesting regular meetings between Anglican and Roman Catholic bishops, through the *ad limina* visits of Roman Catholic bishops to the Pope at regular intervals.[10]

In 1982, all of the statements from ARCIC I, including three *Elucidations*, were gathered together and published under the perhaps rather premature title *ARCIC I The Final Report*. Nevertheless, it was at this point that the process of reception began. The Secretariat (now Council) for Christian Unity in Rome and the Anglican Consultative Council in London sent copies to the bishops of each Church requesting answers to two questions. The first question was: Is the Final Report 'consonant in substance' with the faith of each Church? Secondly, *Anglicans* were asked whether the report 'offers a sufficient basis for taking the next concrete step towards the reconciliation of our Churches grounded in agreement in faith', while *Roman Catholics* were questioned as to 'the agenda for the next stage of this dialogue'. Both Churches responded to these requests in their own different ways. Each of the (then) 29 Anglican provinces was invited to express its judgement in the form of synodical resolutions; these resolutions were summarized in the 1987 *Emmaus Report*. The 1988 Lambeth Conference then passed a resolution in response to this report. The bishops of the Lambeth Conference recognized the Agreed Statements on *Eucharistic Doctrine, Ministry and Ordination* and their *Elucidations* as being 'consonant in substance with the faith of Anglicanism' and they believed that this was a sufficient basis for the next step.[11] They welcomed assurances that further issues be explored and, crucial to the subject in hand, the Conference noted that it:

> welcomes *Authority in the Church* (I and II) together with the *Elucidation* as a firm basis for the direction and agenda of the continuing dialogue on authority and wishes to encourage ARCIC II to continue to explore the basis in Scripture and Tradition of the concept of a universal primacy, in conjunction with collegiality, as an instrument of unity, the character of such a primacy in practice, and to draw upon the experience of other Christian Churches in exercising primacy, collegiality and conciliarity. [12]

This effectively set the agenda that would ultimately lead to the work that is set out in *The Gift of Authority*.

Progress through the appropriate channels in the Roman Catholic Church was slower and ultimately this was to have some effect on later developments within the dialogue. Once again the Vatican received responses from Bishops' Conferences throughout the world. These had been drawn up, following the guidance of the *Observations* of the Congregation of the Doctrine of the Faith (CDF); these *Observations* had been offered in 1982 as the Congregation's 'contribution to this continuing dialogue'. The year 1982 had also seen the visit of Pope John Paul II to the Archbishop of Canterbury at his cathedral during the papal tour of Britain. This meeting both strengthened the resolve of the dialogue and also established a new commission (ARCIC II). The *Official Response* to ARCIC I from the Roman Catholic Church, however, did not appear until 1991. The introductory 'General Evaluation' of this Response gave 'a warm welcome' to *The Final Report* and noted that it 'constituted a significant milestone not only in relations between the Catholic Church and the Anglican Communion but in the ecumenical movement as a whole'.[13] The rest of the *Response* was, however, more critical. It noted further that: 'The Catholic Church judges . . . that it is not yet possible to state that substantial agreement has been reached on all the questions studied by the Commission.'[14] This in itself was unremarkable, since the *Final Report* had itself accepted that there was more work to be done on authority. Nevertheless, the *Response* believed that in the other two areas of study where it was believed agreement had been reached – the Eucharist, and ministry and ordination – further study would be necessary.

ARCIC II debated carefully about how to respond to this. Eventually it did so in a separate document widely known as *Clarifications*, which was published in 1993.[15] This document attempted to answer the questions raised by the *Official Response* and it was offered to the Pontifical Council for Promoting Christian Unity (PCPCU) in this spirit. Once the PCPCU had had time to study *Clarifications*, Cardinal Cassidy, then President of the Pontifical Council, responded with a letter in 1994, the key sentence of which reads: 'The agreement reached on Eucharist and Ministry by ARCIC I is thus greatly strengthened and no further study would seem to be required at this stage.'[16] There remained some questions about Anglican attitudes to the reservation of the Blessed Sacrament. Despite this encouraging reply from the PCPCU, however, a number of events had transpired in the intervening years, which had complicated the dialogue process between the Anglican Communion and the Roman Catholic Church. Although the historic meeting in Canterbury between Archbishop Runcie and Pope John Paul II had given welcome impetus to ARCIC itself, the continuing debate within the Church of England about the ordination of women to the priesthood was viewed gravely by official circles in the Roman Catholic Church. There was a break in the clouds in 1989 with Archbishop Runcie's visit to Pope John Paul II in Rome. Alongside the Common Declaration and after the Pope's homily at Vespers, the Archbishop of Canterbury gave an address. At one key point in this address he offered a reflection, which again is important in setting the context for continued dialogue on authority:

> for the universal Church I renew the plea I made at the Lambeth Conference [1988]: could not all Christians come to reconsider the kind of Primacy the Bishop of Rome exercised within the early Church, a 'presiding in love' for the sake of the unity of the Churches in the diversity of their mission?[17]

Here was the Archbishop of Canterbury calling for a universal primacy, albeit a primacy that would 'preside in love'. This spoke directly to one of the outstanding questions on authority, that of the Petrine Primacy.

Nonetheless, in 1991, the situation became further complicated. The *Official Response* to ARCIC I from the Roman Catholic Church did not seem to reflect the many positive notes which had been struck by many Bishops' Conferences from around the world; indeed there was little overt evidence of any resonance between the Official Response and these other responses. Furthermore, the specific technical issues that had been raised meant that any reply to these criticisms was almost certain to diverge from the now consistent ARCIC methodology which had hitherto avoided reverting to the sixteenth-century disagreements. In the event, in the document *Clarifications* (1993), the Commission was forced to prescind from the method of ARCIC I and re-engage with these historical controversies. As well as seeing the publication of this *Official Response* from the Roman Catholic Church, 1991 also saw the General Synod of the Church of England vote in favour of the ordination of women to the priesthood. Roman Catholic 'official sources' saw this as a new and grave obstacle to unity. Indeed, the issue of the ordination of women to the priesthood and the decision that was made by the members of the General Synod was seen by many primarily not as an issue about ministry but instead about authority. So, a move by the Church of England, mirroring a similar move already taken by other Anglican provinces, notably the Church in the United States of America, in Canada and in New Zealand, raised the issue of the manner of the exercise of authority in the Church through a practical decision on the part of one Church.

Even so, despite the new issues raised both by the Roman Catholic Official Response to ARCIC I and by the Church of England General Synod's decision on the ordination of women to the priesthood, there were still positive signs about the possibilities of ecumenical progress. The publication in 1994 of Pope John Paul II's encyclical on Christian unity, *Ut Unum Sint*, with its call to the Churches to assist him in understanding better the vocation and primacy of the Bishop of Rome, gave those engaged in ecumenical dialogue heart to strive for further agreement. The encyclical noted in relation to the Petrine ministry, in words he had used in a meeting with the late Ecumenical Patriarch, His Holiness Dimitrios I: 'I insistently pray the Holy Spirit to shine his light upon us, enlightening all the Pastors and theologians of our Churches, that we may seek – together, of course – the forms in which this ministry may accomplish a service of love recognised by all concerned.' The encyclical continued: 'Could not the real but imperfect communion existing between us persuade Church leaders and their theologians to engage with me in a patient and fraternal dialogue on this subject .'[18]

In spite of the rather mixed and shifting landscape of the decade running from 1982, when Pope John Paul II visited Canterbury, until 1991 which included both the publication of the Roman Catholic Church's *Official Response* and the vote on the ordination of women in the General Synod, the work of ARCIC proceeded. In 1987 ARCIC II produced its first Agreed Statement, *Salvation and the Church*,[19] responding to the long-term effects of sixteenth-century disagreements and fractures on justification and sanctification. The ARCIC methodology was firmly adhered to, and the 1988 Lambeth Conference responded to the Statement in a provisional but positive manner. The precise wording was that the Conference

> warmly welcomes the first Report of ARCIC II, *Salvation and the Church* (1987), as a timely and significant contribution to the understanding of the Churches' doctrine of salvation and commends this Agreed Statement about the heart of Christian faith to the Provinces for study and reflection.[20]

In 1991 ARCIC II published its second Agreed Statement, *Church as Communion*. This consolidated work on *koinonia* and ecclesiology, and again issues of authority rose unavoidably to the surface:

> We continue to believe that an agreed understanding of the
> Church as communion is the appropriate context in which to
> continue the study of authority in the Church begun by ARCIC I.
> Further study will be needed of episcopal authority, particularly of
> universal primacy, and of the office of the Bishop of Rome; of the
> question of provincial autonomy in the Anglican Communion; and
> the role of the laity in decision-making within the Church.[21]

The Statement begins by rooting its discussion on communion in
Scripture. The terms of reference of *The Gift of Authority* are set out
here implicitly in this mature document on the nature of the Church.

The immediate predecessor document to *The Gift of Authority* within
the work of ARCIC II was the 1994 Agreed Statement, *Life in Christ:
Morals, Communion and the Church*. This was the first document
produced by a bilateral dialogue on morals. At the beginning of
its final section this Statement notes: 'We have already seen how
divergence between Anglicans and Roman Catholics on matters
of practice and official moral teaching has been aggravated, if not
caused, by the historic breach of communion and the consequent
breakdown in communication.'[22] Earlier in the document the
Commission indicates how differing structures of government have
contributed to divergences. There is also a short section on 'Moral
Judgement and the Exercise of Authority'. Towards the end of the
Agreed Statement the Commission makes clear that the fracture
between the two Churches attenuates efforts by the Christian
Church to influence moral decision-making within wider society.
It is clear throughout the document that differences relating to
the nature and exercise of authority are more significant than the
'presenting differences' in teaching in certain areas. It is a lack of
agreement about the nature of authority which makes difficult or
impossible common witness on moral issues within wider society
by our Churches.

As the Commission set to work on *Authority III* they could look back
to, and build upon, the cumulative work of 30 years of constructive
dialogue. Essential to their continuing task is the material of ARCIC I,
which effectively they could count upon as 'banked' within the vaults
of the collective mind of the Anglican–Roman Catholic International
Commission. Despite the sense of unfinished business, ARCIC I
could be proud of its achievement on authority and, indeed, the
manner in which all had been achieved. The ARCIC I statements on
authority, together with the subsequent *Elucidations*, had adhered to
the agreed methodology by reaching back behind the disagreements
of the sixteenth century. Moreover, the Commission deliberately

framed its agreed statement on the preservation of the Church from error without using the word 'infallibility'. In *Authority in the Church II*, the Commission notes of infallibility: 'We agree that this is a term applicable unconditionally only to God, and that to use it of a human being, even in highly restricted circumstances, can produce many misunderstandings. That is why in stating our belief in the preservation of the Church from error we have avoided using the term.' Even reference to Roman Catholic doctrine on this matter is dealt with by using a footnote.[23] *The Gift of Authority*, however, *did not prescind* from using this term of the Church in the main text of the document and this has indeed provoked controversy and some reaction.[24] Even in this area of complexity, ARCIC I had managed to achieve a wide degree of consensus.

Held within the compass of the two earlier agreed statements on authority and the elucidation was a broad area of consensus which could be carried forward as a foundation upon which *Authority III* could be constructed. The first statement concluded that agreement had been reached on authority and the basic principles of primacy. In its section VI, *Problems and Prospects*,[25] some detailed issues relating to papal claims were raised where it was realized that further discussion would be essential. These issues included the Petrine texts, the term 'divine right' used in the First Vatican Council of 1870, universal immediate jurisdiction[26] and infallibility.

The *1981 Elucidation* responded to concerns about whether sufficient attention had been paid to the use of Scripture. This was addressed,[27] as was the area of Councils and Reception. Issues of primacy were further explored and *Authority in the Church II* picked up on the four outstanding problems outlined above. Alongside the issue of infallibility, which we have mentioned, this statement was able to conclude:

> We have already been able to agree that conciliarity and primacy are complementary (*Authority I, s. 22-23*). We can now affirm that the Church needs both a multiple, dispersed authority, with which all God's people are actively involved, and also a universal primate as servant and focus of visible unity in truth and love.[28]

This brought together the role of the laity with universal primacy and both these issues are revisited in more detail in *The Gift of Authority*. ARCIC I's two agreed statements and its elucidation on authority, then, provided both the foundations and launch pad, so to speak, for the work of ARCIC II as it looked to preparing a further agreed statement, *Authority III*.

The situation within our world and within wider culture has changed radically in the forty years since the beginning of the Anglican–Roman Catholic Dialogue, which we can effectively date from Archbishop Fisher's visit to Pope John XXIII in 1960. Although some of the philosophical trends have now shifted and changed – existentialism, for example, is no longer realistically a potent intellectual force – nevertheless, the process of relativization has increased. The apparently opposite trends of fragmentation and globalization have raised more radical questions about the nature of authority both within and beyond the Churches. Few cultures are now homogeneous and Christianity increasingly finds itself set within a broader context alongside other great world religions and increasingly within a secular non-religious context. The cluster of contemporary intellectual trends, loosely described as 'postmodernism', hint at a still more radical diffusion of authority; in its most extreme form such thinking implies a complete 'privatization' of authority within each individual. The polarization of the world into East and West characterized by the Cold War has admittedly disappeared with the collapse of the Soviet Empire. Nevertheless, it has given way to still greater uncertainty, as newly emergent cultures struggle to articulate their identity and as Islam, in particular, seeks to understand how it may relate both to individual nation states and to the present world order.

These radical changes have not removed the need to address issues of authority within the Christian Churches, nor have they necessarily changed the key presenting issues. They have, however, meant a significant change in context for the Christian faith itself. Now the certainties and objectivities, previously assumed from within the bounds of a Western culture that has never fully digested the death of Christendom, must at the very least be argued for – such certainties can no longer be taken for granted by the Churches. Western nations (with the possible exception of the United States of America) have become dominated by an increasingly secularized culture with fewer people attending the churches. Even the change in atmosphere on Good Friday and on Sundays in England over the past 30 years, for example, is an indicator of the different place that religion now assumes within the contemporary world. In what might loosely be described as a 'deregulated society', religion and religious thought have to vie with a great variety of other cultural influences and pressures. The retail revolution has left its invasive imprint here, too. This shift will mean that the ways in which theologians address differences between the Churches and the varying polities within

Christian communities will themselves alter. Indeed, the varied responses to *The Gift of Authority* in this collection mirror both a greater fragmentation within the thought patterns of our society and also the different priorities that may be placed on moves towards unity by different commentators. There is no doubt that the feeling of 'ecumenism being in the air' characterized by the 'heady days' of the 1960s has now passed. There is now, admittedly, perhaps a greater implicit assumption amongst most Christians of a broad unity of purpose. On the other hand, there is less agreement about which methodology and which priorities should order efforts toward the reconciliation of a still critically fractured Christian family.

It may be that *The Gift of Authority* and reactions to it are indicators of the need to address a new and radically different cultural climate. Has that fresh atmosphere first breathed in the 1960s now been stirred up into a more tumultuous series of atmospheric cross-currents? Certainly some have responded fairly sharply and negatively to *The Gift of Authority*. It may be that this radically changed cultural context means that conventional theological approaches to these issues now seem more dramatically counter-cultural than they might have appeared a generation ago. *The Gift of Authority* is the response of ARCIC II to a question set by those who originally established the formal dialogue more than 30 years earlier. This question has been further refined, following the work of ARCIC I on authority. The nuances and lacunae which issued from those earlier statements have gradually fallen more clearly into place, although new and broader challenges have presented themselves to the Churches. The need to confront the outstanding issues from the earlier statements on authority and the need to do so within the context of Scripture (again as argued in earlier agreed statements) is addressed in the key image that shapes the document, the motif of God's 'Yes' to his people, and their 'Amen' in response to his new creation in Christ. We can only understand the aims and conclusions of this most recent ARCIC statement if we read it both within the context of the work of the Commission as a whole and in the light of the radical changes in the nature of wider culture pervading a now 'globalized' world.

chapter two
authority: gift or threat?

Mary Tanner

introduction

Each of us comes to the subject of authority with a mixture of
thoughts and emotions. These will depend on our own experience of
receiving and exercising authority in a variety of contexts – the family,
school, work, the Church, or State. We are each affected by our own
temperament according to whether we are by nature conformist or
non-conformist. Some will have been influenced by growing up in
the 1940s or 1950s with their unquestioning acceptance of authority,
and some by growing up in the 1960s or early 1970s with the
rebelliousness of student riots and protest. Others may have
been influenced by the backlashes that followed the resurgence
of fundamentalisms of different kinds, or by the more recent climate
of postmodernism with its rejection of all authority except my
own authority. Many of us when we hear the word authority will
instinctively think of abusive, coercive power. But if society or the
Churches are to function then, in the words of Robert Runcie,
there is an 'inevitability' about authority.[1] For individuals to live
in relationship in ways that are not destructive, some exercise of
authority is required. So, the authority question is not whether there
should be authority but, rather, what sort of authority and how, and
by what means, is it to be exercised?

This is a question both for the secular world and for the Churches.
Indeed, there is hardly a Church today that does not struggle with
the question of authority. Most Churches are currently confronted
by questions about the uniqueness of Jesus Christ, by issues in the
area of human sexuality, genetic engineering, as well as matters of
ecology. As new and incredibly complex issues arise in the areas of
faith, order or moral life there are bound to be questions about who
discerns and who decides what is right or wrong. What sources are
used in coming to a decision? Who articulates the mind of the group
and what sort of response is expected or required from the group?

Nor is the matter of authority only a concern of individual Churches.
The ecumenical movement has for some decades pledged itself to
the goal of visible unity. It has described that goal as a unity in faith,

in sacraments and ministry, with common ways of deciding and teaching with authority.[2] We may question how many Churches would actually subscribe to this portrait of unity, with its constituent elements of communion, but this is the portrait described by the most inclusive ecumenical forum that exists, the World Council of Churches. Great strides have been made in explicating the common faith, and convergence, even consensus, has been reached in the areas of baptism, Eucharist and ministry.[3] But again and again the ecumenical community has shied away from tackling the third element of visible unity, the exercise of authority. Talk about the Church and authority seems to conjure up a monolithic structure in which diversity is stifled by an authoritarian hierarchy keeping under control an erring laity, a picture hardly compatible with a grace-filled community. And yet, if Christians are to live together in unity – in a communion of faith, life and common mission – if they are to live interdependently and not independently, then the subject of authority cannot be ignored. Moreover, it is an important matter, for the way Christians exercise authority is, or could be, as the Bishop of Truro, the Right Reverend Bill Ind, commented in an article in the *Church Times*, a model for the world's exercise of authority. The subject of authority cannot be avoided either by individual Churches or by an ecumenical fellowship trying to envisage the sort of life that God calls Christians to live together in and for the world.

The fact that Anglicans and Roman Catholics, in our international unity conversations, have ventured together into the area of authority, not once but three times in the last 25 years, is important not only for the two Communions themselves but also for the wider ecumenical movement. Today there is no such thing as an isolated two-partner conversation. What Anglicans and Roman Catholics say to one another must be no different from what they would each say to their other ecumenical partners. Without coherence and consistency in ecumenical conversations there would be chaos in the one ecumenical movement. So the ARCIC agreed statements on authority have implications not only for Anglicans and Roman Catholics but also for the wider ecumenical fellowship.

The Gift of Authority

The Gift of Authority, Authority III was published in 1999.[4] The report builds on the two earlier statements on authority, which were published in 1982 as part of *The Final Report* of the Anglican–Roman Catholic International Commission.[5] It has also taken account of the responses of the two Communions to that earlier work.[6] But *The Gift of Authority* is not simply an elucidation or clarification of those matters raised in the responses of the two Communions. It is a holistic treatment of the subject of authority and stands as a complete document in its own right and must be assessed as such.

The title *The Gift of Authority* immediately strikes a healing note drawing the subject of authority into the realm of divine grace, away from threat. Whether it succeeds in presenting authority as gift must be judged at the end of the exploration. Certainly, many of the immediate reactions that greeted its publication were not convinced that here was a presentation of authority as gift. 'Have Anglicans caved in to the role of the Pope in the Church?' (*Church of England Newspaper*); 'Protestants Betrayed' (Stephen Hampton in *The Tablet*); 'Document trying to divert Anglican Communion from the Via Media to the Via Romana' (Hans Küng in *The Tablet*); 'ARCIC goes too far' (Church of Ireland Gazette); 'From highjackers to highjacked; How ARCIC was captured' (Colin Buchanan in the Church of England Evangelical Council's publication); 'No place for a Patriarch' (*Church of England Newspaper*). These are enough examples to show how high feelings run and what gut reactions are elicited when the subject is authority. But there were other gentler and more welcoming headlines: 'What has been achieved is amazing' (Clifford Longley in the *Independent*); 'A text to ponder' (Henry Chadwick in *The Tablet*).

The Gift of Authority is closely argued. Each sentence builds upon the previous one. It is not easy to summarize the report without damaging the logical progression of the argument. The report requires reading and re-reading if the meaning of the text is to be grasped. My own view of the report is still developing and over at least one crucial issue I do not pretend to have reached a final verdict.

the end of the report first

It may seem strange to begin with paragraphs 53–5, which stand near the end of the report. But there is a reality about these paragraphs, a down-to-earthness about them that makes them a good way in to the subject. These paragraphs make quite clear that neither Communion has the exercise of authority right today. In the Roman Catholic Church there appears to be a struggle going on between the Vatican and local churches on a number of current issues, while the Anglican Communion struggles over the issues of lay presidency and the ordination of practising homosexuals, agonizing over how a decision is to be taken. The 1988 Lambeth Conference, perplexed at how Anglicans could make a decision on a matter like the ordination of women that affects the life of the whole

Communion and not just that of an individual province, identified a need to think about how the Anglican Communion makes authoritative decisions on matters that touch the unity of the Communion.[7] Although Anglican instruments of worldwide communion – the Archbishop of Canterbury, the Lambeth Conference, the Anglican Consultative Council, the Primates' Meeting – have considerable authority to influence and support provinces, yet none of these instruments has power to overrule a provincial decision, even if that decision threatens the unity of the Anglican Communion. The Inter-Anglican Theological and Doctrinal Commission worked for ten years on the subject and offered the bishops at Lambeth 1998 its reflections in *The Virginia Report*.[8] Unfortunately the Lambeth Conference gave little in-depth attention to the report. Nevertheless, the bishops did resolve to strengthen the instruments of communion, particularly the role of the Archbishop of Canterbury and the Primates' Meeting.[9] The Conference requested the Primates' Meeting to initiate a study on effective instruments of communion. The fact of the matter is, Anglicans are coming to see that naked autonomy of provinces is not appropriate for a life of communion. Inter-dependence among local churches and among provinces has to be fostered and maintained. This requires effective instruments of communion and authority, at every level of the Church's life, including at the world level.

Anglicans have not got the exercise of authority right and they acknowledge that fact. Neither, as *The Gift of Authority* says, has the Roman Catholic Church got it right and it also recognizes that that is so. This is why since Vatican II the Roman Catholic Church has been developing synodical structures, in national and regional Episcopal Conferences and in the Assemblies of the Synod of Bishops. At local level, canonical regulation now requires that lay men and women play a part in parochial and diocesan conferences and synods. A leader column in *The Tablet* entitled 'Out of Balance' described the situation:

> As the Catholic Church enters the third millennium, no internal question is more important than how to achieve the right balance between unity and diversity – between the authority of the centre and the authority of local churches . . . It will always be difficult to get the balance right. Pope John Paul II has won his immense authority and prestige by exalting his own office, but there has been a cost which has been paid by his brothers in the episcopate.

And the laity might add, 'a cost also paid by the laity'.

So *The Gift of Authority* is aware that neither Communion has got the exercise of authority right. If Anglicans are 'soggy at the centre', to quote the former Anglican Co-Chairman of ARCIC, if they don't have 'teeth that can bite', Rome has the opposite problem, a centralized system that many experience as an oppressive hierarchical model of authority. Neither Communion has either persons, or structures, or dynamic processes that are authentically effective. To have admitted this in an introduction to the report would have made readers immediately sympathetic to the search for a reformed joint exercise of authority in the Church.

what does *The Gift of Authority* offer?

So, what has the report to offer two Communions that are in trouble with the exercise of authority? In two substantial chapters, Chapters II and III, the report explores first, the place of authority in the Church and second, the actual exercise of authority in the Church. It is important to remember in assessing this text that all ecumenical convergence/ consensus texts are 'ideal' statements about the Church. They are not actual descriptions of the Church today, warts and all. The fact that this is an ideal statement has both advantages and disadvantages. One advantage is that it provides Anglicans and Roman Catholics with something to aim at, something to measure present weaknesses and failures by. However, it can also produce a feeling of cynicism, inviting the response 'this is a Rolls-Royce ecclesiology – things could never really be like that in an imperfect, fallen world'.

the place of authority in the Church (7–31)

Paragraphs 7–13 on the place of authority in the Church set the scene very well for understanding how authority might be exercised in the Church in the future. The chapter contains a grand vision, the grand scheme of things. God's purpose in creation and redemption is to bring all people, all things, into relationship, into communion, with God in a transformed creation. The major image used to describe the relationship here is imaginative and thought-provoking. It has to be grasped if the argument is to be followed. It is the theme of God's 'yes' to humanity and humanity's response of 'Amen' to God. This is a Pauline image taken from Corinthians (2 Corinthians 1.18-20). Creation and redemption are God's way of saying 'yes' to humanity. What God has done in creation and redemption invites a human response of 'Amen' to God. In responding to God in the affirmative the relation of communion with God is maintained. In the sending of Jesus we see God's 'yes' to humanity, God's affirmation of humanity.

In Jesus we also see the perfect human response of 'Amen' to God's purpose. Through the Holy Spirit working in us, we, with Christ, are enabled to say 'Amen', 'yes', to God's purpose for us. The purpose of authority in the Church can be understood in the perspective of God's 'yes' to humanity and the challenge to humanity to respond to God with 'Amen'. Authority in the Church is given to keep the Church remembering God's 'yes' to his people and also to guide the people's response of 'Amen' to God. In other words, authority is to keep the Church faithful in its relationship to God. Or put another way, authority is given to maintain the divine human relationship, to maintain communion. This is a thoroughly biblical perspective in which to reflect upon the place of authority in the Church. Authority is God's gift to the Church, to keep the Church both mindful of God's purpose in creation and redemption, and also to help the Church to respond faithfully to that purpose. This grand scheme of things is an important context in which to set the exploration of how authority works in the Church.

Secondly, this chapter presents an attractive portrait, or model, of the Church in which authority is exercised. It is not a hierarchical model, a top-down model. The report begins with the local church; the place where the individual Christian is formed (11). The report is surely right to insist that our individual response, our individual 'yes' to God is always related to, and set within, the local community of faith. The word that is the basis of our act of faith comes to us through the local community, baptism is a sacrament of the community, and the faith of the individual is nourished in the ongoing life of the local community of faith. The local church is where the individual is formed. But the local church is never isolationist. It is always related to all local churches, across the world and through time. So, the individual Christian makes a response to God's 'Yes' within the community of the local church but also in the communion of all the local churches. In this way individual Christians are locked into the life of the whole Church. The individual response of faith is made in the local church but belongs with the response of the whole Church.

Thirdly, this chapter presents a dynamic picture of the life of the Church, describing the Church living from generation to generation in the Tradition of the Apostles (14). Tradition is not simply a set of propositions, it is the whole life of the Church – the faith, the sacraments, the leadership, the Christian life. The Church constantly receives the Tradition, lives in the Tradition, and passes it on. The Church is called to be faithful in its receiving and its handing on of

Tradition. Nevertheless, it is free to receive the Tradition in new ways according to new situations. Because of human frailty and sin, parts of the Tradition at times may become obscured or simply forgotten, or even rejected. Tradition then has to be rediscovered. This is an extraordinarily important section for Anglicans and for all those Churches that sprang from the Reformation. The Reformation was about just this, the recovering of what had become obscured. It involved a re-reception of the Tradition.

In its discussion of Tradition the Commission had to do some fence mending. It had to reassure evangelical Anglicans in particular, about the place and the authority of Holy Scripture in relation to Tradition. The report explains that: 'Within Tradition the Scriptures occupy a unique and normative place and belong to what has been given once for all'(19). There may be some Anglicans who are not happy with the phrase 'within Tradition'. They will want to hear that Scripture is outside Tradition and above Tradition. But what the report says is thoroughly consonant with ecumenical convergence on this theme. It makes reference to the ecumenical breakthrough on Scripture and Tradition arrived at in the Fourth World Conference on Faith and Order in Montreal in 1963.[10] The chapter could hardly have been stronger in its claims that 'all things are to be measured by Scripture'; and 'the canon is the rule'; and again, 'this corpus alone is the inspired Word of God'; and 'Scripture is uniquely authoritative'.

The emphasis on Scripture provides the opportunity for the report to point out that in the Scriptures themselves we can already see the process of a community receiving the faith and passing it on – the process of reception and re-reception was there from the very beginning of the Church. As the Gospel message is passed on in relation to contemporary situations and conflicts, response is made to them and the community is involved in an ongoing process of reception and re-reception. This thought is hospitable to the way Anglicans see things. It lies behind the Anglican belief that there is development in the life of the Church. But there is a question lurking here, waiting to be answered. Who says what is legitimate development? We have to wait until the next chapter for an answer to that question.

So, the chapter is building up a picture of the Church in God's purposes, sustaining a life of communion with God, living dynamically within the Tradition and out of the Tradition, with Holy Scripture as normative. The picture emphasizes not only the dynamic quality of the Church's life but also the place of diversity in the life of the Church. Again this will resonate with Anglicans. The diversity of human life, given in creation, produces diverse reactions to the Gospel. Moreover, 'the Church's fidelity and identity require not uniformity of expression and formulation at all levels in all situations, but rather catholic diversity within the unity of communion'(27). Here, the authority question is again raised. Who says what is tolerable diversity and who defines the limits to diversity? Again, an answer only comes in the next chapter. But the beginnings of an answer found here are promising. We are told that the whole people of God are the bearers of the living tradition (28); that discernment and communication are the duty of all; that each person has a sense of faith, *sensus fidei* (29), and that when all together exercise in concert their *sensus fidei*, then the *sensus fidelium* is revealed. A fuller treatment of *sensus fidelium* and how it is to be recognized would have been very helpful. It clearly does not mean a majority vote but is more like when a good chairman senses the mind of a meeting.

The chapter ends with a lovely picture of the Church as a great symphony, in which everyone has a part to play. Those with oversight, the theologians and the whole people of God all belong together, and each has a special responsibility in the exercise of authority in the Church. There is a balance in the exercise of authority between the role of the whole people and the role of those with what the report calls 'the ministry of memory'. This is a suggestive phrase and is related to the main theme of God's 'yes' and our 'Amen'. Those with a ministry of memory are those called to remind the Church of God's affirmation of humanity in creation and redemption, and also to remind the Church of humanity's vocation to respond with 'Amen' to God's calling.

This crucial scene-setting chapter ends by assuring the reader that neither Communion has got the exercise of authority right. Each has to re-receive the Tradition and today there is everything to be gained by re-receiving it together. There is no capitulation of Anglicans to Roman Catholics or vice versa.

The chapter has presented a picture, admittedly an ideal one, of the Church and its place in the purposes of God. The Church is both local and universal. It is called to live dynamically in the Tradition from generation to generation, receiving and re-receiving the Tradition, with Scripture as normative. The Church is characterized by rich diversity. This is the Church to which God gives the gift of authority to help the Church live faithful to God's 'yes' to humanity. The whole Church bears the responsibility for discovering truth and maintaining faithfulness. But within the Church there is a special ordained ministry of memory.

There can be few Anglicans, or indeed other Christians from the mainline Churches, who would not agree with most of this and find much in it to give them confidence about authority in the Church and the unique role of Holy Scripture. There have been some very welcome things said to dispel the fears of those who are afraid of an authoritarian hierarchical model of the Church, not least of all that is said about the place of the local church and the role of the laity. If this is the Church in which authority is to be exercised then surely authority will be experienced as gift? But there have also been questions awaiting an answer. Who, when the chips are down, decides what is legitimate development? Who, when the chips are down, says what is tolerable diversity? And what are the structures and processes of discernment through which authority is mediated?

the exercise of authority in the Church (32–50)

In paragraphs 32–50 the report turns to examine some of these questions as it turns to the exercise of authority in the Church. This is where, as one commentator has said, the real dynamite lies. The section begins with another helpful image that sums up what has gone before. The Church is called to 'walk together on the way', *syn-hodos*. Synodality, the being together on the way, encapsulates a vital truth about the life of the Church. Synodality is not merely about structures. It describes the mode of the Church's life. It is a good image because it emphasizes togetherness, in the same way as the image of the symphony did. At the same time, synodality also entails dynamic movement in the life of the Church.

This chapter once more begins by emphasizing the local church with its bishop. The bishop is the one entrusted with 'the ministry of memory and teaching' (41). This reminds readers again of the need to remember the Tradition of God's 'yes' to humanity and the challenge to humanity to respond with 'Amen'. The bishop is the one to whom the ministry of oversight is given in order to implement decisions for the sake of maintaining communion, *koinonia*. The bishop is the one who links the local church to the rest of the Church, through membership of the college of bishops. The bishop brings the insights and concerns of the local church to the gatherings of the bishops in the college of bishops. In the college, the bishops, the ones who are entrusted with the 'ministry of memory and teaching', act together to discern and to articulate the mind of all the faithful. Anglicans, indeed any church with a ministry of oversight, whatever those ministers of oversight are called, should have no problem with the notions of either personal or collegial oversight (*episcope*) outlined here. The multilateral report from the Faith and

Order Commission of the World Council of Churches, *Baptism, Eucharist and Ministry* (BEM), describes three aspects of ministry – personal, collegial and communal.[11] In the same way, *The Gift of Authority* describes both the personal and collegial ministry of bishops. It also refers to synodal gatherings of bishops with lay people. This is close to what BEM calls the communal dimension of ministry. *The Gift of Authority* refers to the fact that both the Anglican Communion and the Roman Catholic Church are currently struggling to understand how best in practice these different aspects, or dimensions, of the ministry of oversight relate to one another in the exercise of authority (38–40).

At this point Anglicans might want to ask for more clarity on the relation between collegial gatherings of those entrusted with oversight – meetings of bishops – and synodical gatherings involving the laity. They might want to press the questions: At what levels of the Church's life are synodical gatherings involving the laity appropriate? What is their precise role in the exercise of authority? When the chips are down, are synods with lay members no more than sounding boards for the bishops who then decide to take their advice or leave it? The report seems to suggest that this is so when it says that the role of the bishops 'is magisterial: that is, in this communion of the churches, **they** are to determine what is to be taught as faithful to the apostolic Tradition'. Are the bishops in the end the ones who have the authority to decide? What then is the precise role of the laity in synods if decisions are taken in the college and not in synods?

Now we come to what are surely the most crucial paragraphs of the report. Paragraphs 42 and 43 require the most careful attention: they aim to explain precisely how the Holy Spirit keeps the whole Church 'faithful to apostolic Tradition'. Anglicans would surely welcome the fact that discernment belongs to the whole Church. They might want to be assured about how this works out in practice. How is the whole Church involved in discernment? They would have no objection to saying that bishops have a special role to discern the mind of the Church and to teach. They would also surely welcome the view that new formulations have to be tested against Scripture and Tradition. But they might just want to pause for a moment at this thought:

> In specific circumstances, those with this ministry of oversight (*episcope*), assisted by the Holy Spirit, may together come to a judgement which, being faithful to Scripture and consistent with apostolic Tradition, is preserved from error. By such a judgement, which is a renewed expression of God's one 'Yes' in Jesus Christ, the Church is maintained in the truth so that it may continue to

> offer its 'Amen' to the glory of God. This is what is meant when it is affirmed that the Church may teach *infallibly* . . . Such infallible teaching is at the service of the Church's indefectibility. (42)

It is important to note that it is the Church that 'may teach infallibly'. Anglicans will not be the only ones to pause over this and ask: But what are the 'specific circumstances'? Indeed, are there ever any circumstances in which, when the bishops speak, the only response must be one of immediate acceptance? Would not Anglicans want to say that whenever the bishops speak, their teaching still has to be received by the whole Church? What if the people say 'no' and vote with their feet? The report in another place does say that individual conscience must be respected (49). But is there also a place for group conscience and dissent that might, in certain circumstances, challenge and even change the mind of the bishops? If so, how would it be known when an episcopal judgement was preserved from error without some form of testing?

Before jumping to conclusions about what is said in paragraph 42, a careful examination needs to be made of what the report goes on to say in the following paragraph. Paragraph 43 claims that the whole body of believers, together with those who have the ministry of memory, take part in the discernment. Moreover, authoritative definitions are received as authoritative because of the office of the persons, or person, who proclaim the *sensus fidelium*. 'When the people of God respond by faith and say "Amen" to authoritative teaching it is because they recognise that this teaching expresses the apostolic faith.' The implication in this circular argument is that when the bishops, after careful listening to the faithful, proclaim what they have discerned as the *sensus fidelium* and have assured themselves that this is consonant with Scripture and Tradition, then the response of the faithful to what the bishops teach must inevitably be 'Amen'. The people will indeed recognize the truth. But can we ever be completely certain that what the bishops have discerned and are teaching is consonant with Scripture and Tradition without assessing that teaching? If we were assured that that were guaranteed to be so, then automatic acceptance of a teaching as being infallible would surely be right. But who says that the teaching of the bishops is, even in certain circumstances, guaranteed to be consonant with Scripture and Tradition? What does the history of the Church suggest? The report itself would answer that the bishops only speak after they have discerned the *sensus fidelium* and after they have assured themselves that the teaching is consonant with Scripture and Tradition. No further testing or discernment by the faithful is; therefore, required, no further 'open reception' is necessary. Reception has already taken place within the discernment process itself as the bishops received the *sensus fidelium* from the faithful. In assessing this argument it needs to be remembered that this is an 'ideal' statement.

Nevertheless, Anglicans might still want to satisfy themselves on this point because this was one of the major issues raised by the Church of England in its response to the earlier work of the first Commission. *Authority II* included the sentence:'If the definition proposed for assent were not manifestly a legitimate interpretation of biblical faith and in line with orthodox tradition, Anglicans would think it a duty to reserve the reception of the definition for study and discussion.'[12] The Anglican members of ARCIC I obviously thought that there might be statements that were not consonant with Scripture and Tradition.

There are questions that remain. Under what circumstances can we be assured that bishops discern the *sensus fidelium*? And under what circumstances do bishops, by virtue of office, judge in accordance with Scripture and Tradition? In an ideal world they always would – and this report is an ideal picture. But what about in the messiness of history? Is there not a balance to be struck between, on the one hand, the right confidence the laity can rightly be expected to have in those whom Christ, through the Church, calls to exercise oversight, and, on the other hand, the awareness of the reality of human frailty and sin? There is the power God gives to guide the Church but there is also the power of human sin to distort God's gift. The Church on earth lives in the tension of these opposing realities. The Church is called to live trusting in the power of the Holy Spirit to lead into all truth, expecting all to be well. But the Church has also to live in the knowledge of the human capacity to frustrate God's plan. Blind trust may be as dangerous as a lack of trust. For this reason it may not be enough to say that discernment of the *sensus fidelium* and reception takes place only before declaration. It may be that a process of reception by the whole Church should also, in a sinful world, follow declaration by the college of bishops. Paragraphs 42 and 43 are not easy to understand, even after many readings. It could be that if a description of how this might work out in a particular instance could be given, then it would be not only clear but also quite acceptable.

There is another question that Anglicans may wish to raise at this point and that is the use of the word 'infallible'. It is important that it is the Church that may 'teach infallibly', rather than any one person (42). Nevertheless, the word carries much baggage with it. It may not be any easier to re-content this word than it has been to re-content the word 'transubstantiation' in the discussions on the Eucharist.

The wisdom of ecumenical conversation is usually to leave polarized language of past polemics behind and to express common beliefs in fresh language that is less capable of being misunderstood. Moreover, Anglicans in dialogue with other Churches have rejected the use of the term infallible, as have some of our other partners in dialogue with the Roman Catholic Church. Whether *The Gift of Authority* has in fact succeeded in providing a way of reclaiming the word 'infallible', applying it to the Church, will need very careful assessment in the process of responding to this report. That the Holy Spirit will lead the Church into all truth is one thing. Anglicans uphold a belief in the indefectibility of the Church. But the capacity of individuals and institutions to resist that leading from time to time is another. Are we not called to live together in the confident expectation that those chosen to lead will indeed discern what is the mind of Christ and yet, at the same time, engage in a process of reflection on their teaching, while the whole Church affirms – or indeed rejects – that teaching? Nevertheless, there are some sharp questions that Anglicans will need to ask themselves. Not least of all whether a process of discernment and reception on a matter of order or morals requires restraint in action until the Church comes to a common mind. But restraint would only be a credible option if dialogue were openly encouraged, indeed managed by those with oversight, as part of the reception process.

primacy and the ministry of the Bishop of Rome (45–8)

Anglicans are familiar to some degree with a ministry of primacy both at the level of provinces and at the world level with the ministry of the Archbishop of Canterbury. The ministry of universal primacy of the Bishop of Rome is presented in the report as gift to the Church. Many Anglicans will be happy to agree this, or at least to say that in a re-formed fashion it could be. The recent invitations of the Bishop of Rome to heads of other Churches to join him in praying for peace in Assisi, or to open with him the Holy Door in St Peter's Basilica at the start of a new millennium, show something of the potential of a universal ministry in the service of reconciliation and unity. The report is surely right to insist that a personal ministry of unity and reconciliation at the world level is gift. The report is clear that this ministry of primacy has to be exercised collegially with all the bishops. It insists that when the Bishop of Rome speaks, together with the college of bishops, he does not speak his own private faith (47). When the Bishop of Rome speaks, he proclaims the faith of the local churches as that which has been represented in the college by those whose task it is to present the faith of their local church. It is the reliable teaching of the whole Church that is operative in a judgement of the universal primate. That the college requires a primate who can speak on its behalf is clear. However, the report is less clear when it claims that in certain circumstances, the Bishop of Rome has a duty 'to discern and make explicit'. If this is simply like any good chairperson saying to a meeting, 'this is what I hear you saying', then this is surely a proper role for a president of a college of bishops, a servant of the servants of God. But, if this discernment and making explicit is understood to be a personal judgement, even if only in certain circumstances, then Anglicans might be less than happy.

But, what is very striking is that the report does not use the word 'infallible' of the ministry of the Bishop of Rome. Infallible teaching is used of the teaching of the whole Church in this report. This should encourage Anglicans. However, the same question remains as in the case of the college of bishops – when the Bishop of Rome in certain circumstances 'discerns and makes explicit', ought that not to require reception by the whole Church and not automatic acceptance?

The House of Bishops of the Church of England, in its response to the Bishop of Rome's invitation to help him understand his ministry in the service of the unity of the Church, a remarkable invitation that went out to all the churches in the papal encyclical *Ut Unum Sint*, quoted what had been said in the Church of England's response to ARCIC I:

> It would be one thing for Anglicans to say 'yes' to the universal primacy of the bishop of Rome as the person who particularly signifies the unity and universality of the Church and to acknowledge his special responsibilities for maintaining unity in truth and ordering things in love; it would be quite another to agree to infallibility without the understanding of reception as we have described it.[13]

There are questions needing further exploration and explication about the infallible teaching of the Church expressed by the college of bishops, and, within that, the specific teaching ministry of the Bishop of Rome. As the report itself so rightly acknowledges, authority is exercised by fragile Christians for the sake of fragile Christians (48). Does not this very fragility require an ongoing process of reception following the definition of a doctrine, either by the college or by the one who presides over the college? But even when these questions have been identified it is evident that the report has made a significant advance in understanding the ministry of authority in the Church.

challenges to both Communions (56–63)

The report ends with a series of challenges, first to each Communion. Next there are challenges to be faced together and, then, one final explosive challenge. The challenges to both Communions are on target. Anglicans are asked to consider whether the Anglican Communion is open to the acceptance of instruments of oversight, which would allow decisions to be made that in certain circumstances would call for restraint or even bind the whole Communion. They are challenged to consider to what extent does unilateral action by provinces or dioceses in matters concerning the whole Church, even after consultation, weaken *koinonia*. The Roman Catholic Church is challenged to consider the participation of the laity in the life and structures of the Church, whether collegiality has been properly implemented after *Vatican II*, whether there is enough consultation between the Bishop of Rome and the local churches, whether the variety of theological opinion is taken into account, and whether the structures and procedures of the Roman Curia adequately respect the exercise of oversight at other levels. Challenges to be faced together include implementing ways of 'cooperating and developing relationships of mutual accountability in the exercise of oversight' (58). Suggestions made include bishops meeting together regularly, locally and regionally, Anglican bishops joining *ad limina* visits to Rome, joint episcopal teaching in matters of faith and order, and sharing oversight in local matters. It is striking that for all the report's stress on the synodality of the life of the Church, in which those with oversight work with all the people, no joint challenge is addressed to the laity. Could it not be that there are ways even now where laity might share in the synods and councils of the other Church?

Finally comes the most daring challenge of all. The challenge to both Communions to what the report calls 're-receive' the ministry of the Bishop of Rome. Not only the Anglican Communion but the Church of Rome is asked to re-receive that ministry. Both are to re-receive the ministry of the Bishop of Rome, a ministry of primacy exercised in collegiality, and synodality – a ministry of the servant of the servants of God, a primacy that would uphold diversity and encourage mission. The picture is an attractive one. The Commission says in paragraph 60:

> We envisage a primacy that will even now help to uphold the legitimate diversity of traditions, strengthening and safeguarding them in fidelity to the Gospel.

Paragraph 61 continues:

> Such a universal primate will exercise leadership in the world
> and also in both communions, addressing them in a prophetic
> way. He will promote the common good in ways that are not
> constrained by sectional interests . . . A universal primacy of
> this style will welcome and protect theological enquiry and other
> forms of the search for truth so that their results may enrich and
> strengthen both human wisdom and the Church's faith. Such a
> universal primacy might gather the churches in various ways for
> consultation and discussion.

The report's major and startling conclusion is 'that Anglicans be
open to and desire a recovery and re-reception under certain clear
conditions of the exercise of universal primacy by the Bishop of
Rome' and 'that Roman Catholics be open to and desire a re-
reception of the exercise of primacy by the Bishop of Rome and
the offering of such a ministry to the whole Church of God'(62).
The further startling suggestion is made that such a primacy could
be offered and received even before the establishment of full
communion. This is a bold suggestion and one that deserves the
most serious consideration and response by Anglicans. Could the
Pope, even now, exercise a ministry for Anglicans? It is surely an
attractive suggestion in a world that needs to see unity modelled by
Christians and to hear from them a united message of reconciliation
and love. A personal focus of unity for all Christians would be a
powerful symbol. The gatherings at Assisi have already pointed to
the potential of a ministry of universal primacy. The Church of England
in its response to ARCIC I, while acknowledging the difficulty of a
ministry of infallibility, nevertheless did envisage Anglicans saying yes
'to the universal primacy of the Bishop of Rome as the person who
particularly signifies the unity and universality of the Church'. They
did envisage Anglicans acknowledging his 'special responsibilities for
maintaining unity in the truth and ordering all things in love.'[14]

final reflections

The Gift of Authority is on any reckoning an important contribution
to the understanding of authority in the Church. It has so much that
Anglicans who are committed to discovering how they might live in
visible unity with Roman Catholics will be only too ready to affirm.
This is good news, for as George Carey, Archbishop of Canterbury,
and Pope John Paul II said in their Common Declaration in 1996: 'We
shall not reach full visible unity unless we reach sufficient agreement

over authority.' The report helps us to understand authority as God's gift both to keep the Church mindful of God's 'Yes' to humanity and faithful in responding with 'Amen' to God's purpose. It offers an attractive description of the Church as a dynamic and diverse community walking together on the way, responding to new situations and new questions. It likens the Church to a symphony. There is no room for an oppressive hierarchical model of the Church. The local church is prior, never isolated, but linked in communion with all the local churches across the world and through time. Everyone, the people, theologians and those entrusted with a 'ministry of memory', have roles to play in the exercise of authority, in decision-making and teaching with authority. The ministries of collegiality and primacy belong together, always exercised within the synodality of the whole Church, as the Tradition is received, lived in and passed on with freshness and relevance to new situations. It is hard to read the report and not to be impressed by one or other of its suggestive images or similes, whether it is that of 'God's Yes and our Amen', or 'the symphony', or 'the walking together on the way', or 'the ministry of memory'.

Of course the picture is an ideal one, as are most ecumenical convergence and consensus documents. Nevertheless, *The Gift of Authority* does acknowledge the reality of human sin and weakness: 'Human weakness and sin do not only affect individual ministers: they can distort the human structuring of authority.' For this reason 'loyal criticism and reforms are sometimes needed'(48). It is because this is so that the question has to be pressed: Are there ever circumstances in the real world, 'any special circumstances', in which, when a college has discerned, or the Bishop of Rome has discerned in the college, it can without doubt be said to be the infallible teaching of the Church, without that being confirmed in a positive response, a positive reception by the whole Church? Can we trust that reception has already taken place and consonance with Scripture and Tradition perceived before declaration by the college or the Pope on behalf of the college? We should at least need to know more about what such special circumstances might be and who would determine such circumstances.

What is needed now is a more descriptive and factual map of those persons, structures and processes of discernment, decision-making, proclamation and reception by which authoritative teaching is given. How, for example, in practice, would local churches be held in the communion of all the churches through collegial meetings of bishops and synodical meetings of bishops with laity? Or how would the ministry of primacy work in collegial and synodical gatherings at the different levels of the Church's life? Or what role would administrators and administrative structures play in the life of the Church, local and worldwide? It is important to get some idea of how, in practice, the laity are involved with ordained ministers at the different levels of the life of the Church, and how the different levels interrelate. *The Gift of Authority* takes us a very long way in understanding the sort of Church in which authority will be experienced as gift of God. It provides convincing clues as to how Anglicans and Roman Catholics might live together in visible unity in the future. The responses of the two Communions will help to clarify some of the outstanding issues.

But perhaps the most important thing that this report has done is to identify for both Anglicans and Roman Catholics weaknesses in their own current exercise of authority. If both Communions were able to respond to the challenges by re-forming their own exercise of authority in the ways suggested by the report, then we should find that the two Communions had moved much closer to one another. And if every opportunity can be grasped to exercise authority together now in the ways suggested in this report, then again significant growth to visible unity would take place. Anglicans and Roman Catholics must now hold one another accountable for re-forming both their own lives and for taking steps together. Encouragement and monitoring of re-formation would be an appropriate task for the new International Anglican–Roman Catholic Commission on Unity and Mission set up by the Archbishop of Canterbury and the Pope after the meeting of bishops in Mississauga in May 2000.

Moves to re-form would also provide a good context in which to consider how both Communions might set about re-receiving the ministry of the Bishop of Rome. The two meetings called by the Pope at Assisi in the cause of unity, reconciliation and peace, with the response made by two Archbishops of Canterbury, are already indications of the importance of the role of the Bishop of Rome in the service of unity, peace and reconciliation. Archbishop Robert Runcie, in his address to the bishops at the 1988 Lambeth Conference, reflected on his experience of being at the Assisi gathering in 1986.

> Whether we like it or not there is only one Church, and one bishop, who could have effectively convoked such an ecumenical gathering. At Assisi I saw the vision of a new style of Petrine ministry – an ARCIC primacy rather than a papal monarchy. Pope John Paul welcomed us – including other Anglican primates . . . but then he became in his own words a brother among brothers.[15]

The positive response of Archbishop George Carey to the Pope's invitation to push open with him the Holy Door of the Basilica of St Peter's at the beginning of a new millennium was another important sign of a growing together. It is in events such as these that Anglicans are already beginning to recognize the potential for good of ministry of primacy of the Bishop of Rome and to re-receive that ministry. In their response to the Pope's invitation to help him consider his ministry in the service of the unity of the Church given in *Ut Unum Sint*, the House of Bishops of the Church of England said: 'Anglicans are thus by no means opposed to the principle and practice of a personal ministry at the world level in the service of unity.'[16]

The Gift of Authority takes us a very, very long way in understanding authority and its exercise in the life of the Church. The report deserves careful study, considered response but, above all, well-considered reforming action separately and together now on the way to visible unity.

chapter three

'yes' and 'no' – a response to *The Gift of Authority*

Martin Davie

introduction

As *The Gift of Authority* itself explains, at the heart of what it has to say there is the theme, taken from 2 Corinthians 1.18-20, of God's 'Yes' to humanity and a corresponding 'Yes' or 'Amen' uttered by humanity to God:

> The authority of Jesus Christ is that of the 'faithful witness,' the 'Amen' (cf. Rev 1.5; 3.14) in whom all the promises of God find their 'Yes.' When Paul had to defend the authority of his teaching he did so by pointing to the trustworthy authority of God: 'As surely as God is faithful, our word to you has not been Yes and No. For the Son of God, Jesus Christ, whom we preached among you . . . was not Yes and No; but in him it is always Yes. For all the promises of God find their Yes in him. That is why we utter the Amen through him, to the glory of God' (2 Cor 1.18-20). Paul speaks of the 'Yes' of God to us and the 'Amen' of the Church to God. In Jesus Christ, Son of God and born of a woman, the 'Yes' of God to humanity and the 'Amen' of humanity to God become a concrete human reality. This theme of God's 'Yes' and humanity's 'Amen' in Jesus Christ is the key to the exposition of authority in this statement.[1]

The theme of God's 'Yes' to humanity and humanity's 'Yes' in response is not just an important theme in Christian theology. It is *the* important theme in Christian theology. It is what Christian theology is all about.

This is because at the heart of the Christian faith is the conviction that God has made an eternal decision to say 'Yes' to the entire created order by bringing it into unity with himself through Christ so that it might share his own life for ever (Ephesians 1.10).

In the light of this conviction, the task given to Christian theology is to expound how God's eternal 'Yes' to the created order was reflected in the divine activity to which the Bible bears witness, and what it means to respond appropriately to this activity by saying 'Yes' to God in thought, speech and behaviour.

It is important to note, however, that both God's 'Yes' to the created order and the human 'Yes' to God involve a corresponding 'No'. God's intention to bless the created order involves his saying 'No' to everything that is contrary to that intention, and humanity's calling to obey God means saying 'No' to everything that is contrary to such obedience.

That is why the whole Bible from Genesis to Revelation is full of 'No' as well as 'Yes'. For example, in the creation story with which the Bible begins God says 'No' to humanity eating from the fruit of the tree of the knowledge of good and evil (Genesis 2.16-17), and in the final chapter of the Book of Revelation with which the Bible ends, St John says 'No' to anyone adding to the words of his prophecy (Revelation 22.18-19). In between there is a whole range of 'Nos', from the prohibitions in the Ten Commandments (Exodus 20.2-17) to St Paul's 'No' to those who were undermining his teaching about justification by faith (Galatians 3.1–5.12).

Where the Bible leads, Christian theology has to follow. Saying 'Yes' to God involves saying 'No' to that which is not of God. The challenge facing the Christian is to discern when to say 'Yes' and when to say 'No'. *The Gift of Authority* gives a very straightforward account of the process of discernment. The faithful hear God's 'Yes' mediated via the apostolic Tradition as interpreted through the *sensus fidelium* and expressed by the teaching of the college of bishops headed by the Pope. Having heard God's 'Yes' in this way, the faithful then respond with 'Amen'.

The argument of this chapter is that this account is too straightforward. It does not adequately describe the complexity of hearing God's voice in a world where such hearing is distorted by sin and finitude. As a result, *The Gift of Authority* does not provide an accurate account of how authority is or ought to be exercised in the Church of God.

Therefore while this essay notes that there are many things that *The Gift of Authority* says about the exercise of divine authority in the Church which are helpful and to which we must therefore say 'Yes', it also notes that there are significant areas in which problems remain and concerning which we must therefore say 'No'.

Here also, however, 'No' is said for the sake of saying 'Yes'. The purpose of identifying the problems that remain is not to call into question the search for agreement about authority between the Anglican Communion and the Roman Catholic Church, but to indicate where, from an Evangelical Anglican perspective, more work needs to be undertaken so that agreement can be achieved and we can with good conscience say 'Amen' to each other in the belief that we are at the same time saying 'Amen' to God.

'yes' – eight aspects of *The Gift of Authority* that are helpful

1. Its insistence that authority in the Church is fundamentally evangelical in nature. That is to say, according to *The Gift of Authority*, what Christians are called upon to accept is ultimately the good news of what God has done and will do for the world in Christ. All human forms of authority in the Church are to be accepted because, and in so far as, they make this good news known and enable believers to respond to it in faith.[2]

2. Its insistence on the primacy of Scripture. Part of what has made many Anglicans hostile to Roman Catholic theology has been a suspicion that Rome does not give a proper place to the authority of Scripture as the fundamental norm for all Christian theology. *The Gift of Authority*, however, is quite clear that the Holy Scriptures have a unique authority and are the canon against which the Church must test all that it says and does.[3]

3. The way in which *The Gift of Authority* has developed a comprehensive and dynamic understanding of Tradition. In the past there has been a tendency to see 'tradition' in terms of a series of unchanging dogmatic propositions and ecclesiastical decisions that could potentially be set alongside, and be a rival to, the authority of Scripture. Reflecting much contemporary ecumenical thinking about Tradition, *The Gift of Authority*, however, describes Tradition as being the way in which, through the work of the Holy Spirit, the Gospel witnessed to by Holy Scripture is communicated in all areas of the Church's life, in ways that necessarily change in order to respond to changing cultures and circumstances.[4]

4. The way in which *The Gift of Authority* insists that the exercise of teaching authority in the Church is linked inextricably to the discernment of the meaning of the Gospel message by the people of God as a whole. Another perennial Anglican criticism has been that within Roman Catholicism authority rests only with the

bishops, and ultimately with the Pope, and that the role of the ordinary clergy and laity is simply to submit to their teaching. *The Gift of Authority* makes clear, however, that the teaching of the bishops, including the Bishop of Rome himself, only possesses authority because it embodies that understanding of the Gospel to which all of God's people have been led through the guidance of the Spirit, and is accepted by them as so doing.[5]

5. The explicit recognition that the Tradition of the Church and the teaching of its bishops (including the Bishop of Rome) can be subject to human weakness and sin, and that therefore both the Tradition of the Church and the teaching of its bishops can legitimately be subject to criticism, reformation and renewal. This has been a cardinal principle of Anglicanism since the Reformation, but it has been one which Anglicans have not been sure has been accepted in Roman Catholicism so its enunciation in *The Gift of Authority* has been very welcome.[6]

6. The insistence of *The Gift of Authority* on the fact that the Bishop of Rome is part of the college of bishops and that he possesses authority in that context. Part of the reason why Anglicans have traditionally been hesitant about the authority given to the Bishop of Rome within Roman Catholicism has been a belief that this has been at the expense of the authority that rightly belongs to the whole episcopal college. It is therefore good to see *The Gift of Authority* insisting that the two cannot be set in opposition because the Bishop of Rome can only exercise authority as part of the college of bishops and on its behalf in the same way that the college of bishops itself exercises authority as part of, and on behalf of, the Church as a whole.[7]

7. The description of universal primacy at the end of the report. This description of a form of primacy that would promote the wellbeing of the Church as a whole while upholding a legitimate diversity of traditions and welcoming theological enquiry,[8] reflects the sort of primacy which has developed within Anglicanism and with which Anglicans feel comfortable, as opposed to the more authoritarian style of primacy which they have traditionally associated with Rome.

8. Its suggestion of more co-operation between the bishops of the two Communions as a way of making visible the unity that already exists between them.[9] This sort of co-operation is already taking place in some parts of the world, the regular and fruitful meetings between Church of England bishops and their Roman Catholic

counterparts in almost all parts of England being a good example, and from an Anglican point of view this is certainly something to be encouraged.

'no' – areas in which problems remain

1 the use of the term 'Church'

The first of these areas is the use of the terms 'Church' and 'local church' in Chapters II and III of *The Gift of Authority*. In these chapters, and particularly in Chapter III, the discussion of the transmission of tradition and the exercise of pastoral and teaching authority assumes that both the Church as a whole and the local churches have an episcopal polity. No reference is made to the fact that within the Church of Christ there are many Christian communities that do not have an episcopal polity and in which, nonetheless, the Christian tradition is passed on and in which pastoral and teaching authority is duly exercised.

In its ecumenical conversations and agreements with such communities, and in the sections of its Canon Law regulating its ecumenical involvement, the Church of England has acknowledged both explicitly and implicitly that *they* are part of the one, holy, catholic and apostolic Church[10] and that there is an exercise of *episcope* within them. It would have been better if this fact had been reflected in *The Gift of Authority*.

It is important to recognize the existence of these communities because the fact that, in their case, tradition is transmitted and *episcope* exercised in the absence of bishops raises the question, which *The Gift of Authority* does not consider, about why episcopal ministry is so important if so many Christian communities appear to flourish without it.[11]

This question needs to be discussed because statements about the Christian Church as a whole, which fail to acknowledge the diversity of forms of ministry within it, do not adequately reflect the complex reality of the Church's actual existence.

2 the authority of Tradition

The second of these areas is the question of the authority of Tradition. As has already been noted, *The Gift of Authority* develops a dynamic understanding of Tradition and makes clear that the teaching of Scripture is the norm to which Tradition must conform. All this is welcome from an Anglican point of view.

What is missing, however, is a recognition that in the process of handing on the Gospel from one generation to another in the Church, which is what *The Gift of Authority* seems to mean by Tradition,[12] teaching may emerge which distorts or departs from the teaching of Scripture and is thus a source of error.

As we have noted, *The Gift of Authority* acknowledges that the corporate memory of the people of God can become distorted by finitude and sin, and the solution that is suggested when this occurs is fresh recourse to Tradition. What is not acknowledged is that the way in which Tradition has developed may itself be the problem and needs to be corrected by Scripture. It seems to be assumed within *The Gift of Authority* that Tradition and Scripture will always be in harmony.

Anyone who takes seriously the witness of the New Testament will have difficulty with this suggestion since not only does it contain specific teaching about the way in which the witness of Scripture can be obscured by human tradition (see for example Mark 7.1-23), but in fact the whole basis of New Testament theology is a correction of existing Jewish tradition on the basis of a fresh interpretation of Scripture in the light of Jesus Christ.

In similar fashion, the theologians of the Protestant Reformation, including the theologians of the Anglican Reformation, felt that it was necessary to distinguish between what Thomas Cranmer called 'the well of life in the books of the Old and New Testament' and the 'stinking puddles of men's traditions',[13] because they felt that the teaching of Scripture had become hidden by the Tradition of the Medieval Church, and they too proposed a correction of Tradition on the basis of a Christ-centred interpretation of biblical teaching.

This history is not mentioned in *The Gift of Authority*. It allows that, 'some of the formulations of the Tradition' can be seen as 'inadequate or even misleading in a new context',[14] but it does not admit the simple proposition that some of the formulations of the Tradition may have been wrong all along.

It might be argued that even in the cases cited it would be wrong to put Scripture and Tradition in absolute opposition since both the New Testament and the Protestant Reformation build on aspects of existing Jewish and Catholic belief and practice. This is undoubtedly true, but it highlights another issue raised by the discussion of Tradition in *The Gift of Authority*, which is the assumption that Tradition is uniform.

The Gift of Authority acknowledges the diversity of Christian traditions, describing these as 'diverse expressions' of Tradition. That is to say, there is one Tradition which is expressed in a variety of different ways. The problem with this way of looking at things is that it does not do justice to the fact that many of the expressions of the Christian Tradition contradict each other.

For example, Arianism and some forms of modern liberal Christianity have affirmed that the Son of God is a created being, while Nicene orthodoxy holds that he is part of the Godhead. For another example, Christians in the Orthodox tradition hold that it is a legitimate and very important form of Christian devotion to give reverence to icons, while other Christians have held and continue to hold that this is a breach of the second commandment and therefore impermissible.

It is not possible to regard such differences as simply diverse expressions of Tradition without holding that Tradition itself is self-contradictory. It would therefore have been better if *The Gift of Authority* had contained a discussion of the limits of Christian diversity, and an affirmation that an acceptance of the normative authority of Scripture means following the example of the Christians of the Early Church and Reformation periods by assessing the Tradition of the Christian Church in the light of Scripture and only retaining those elements of Tradition that are consonant with Scripture. As the 1981 *Elucidation* to ARCIC I's first statement on *Authority in the Church* put it, 'since the Scriptures are the uniquely inspired witness to divine revelation, the Church's expression of that revelation must be tested by its consonance with Scripture'.[15]

If Tradition is concerned with the faithful transmission of the Gospel from one generation to the next in the community of the Church then Tradition must be tested by its consonance with Scripture because according to the historic witness of the Church down the centuries it is in the Scriptures that we find the normative prophetic and apostolic witness to the Gospel.

This does not, of course, solve the problem, which the differences between Protestants at the period of the Reformation made clear, of how one decides what is consonant with Scripture and who should make this decision, but it does at least provide the Church's discussion of the issue of Tradition with a correct starting point.

3   the indefectibility of the Church

The third area in which problems remain is what is said about the 'indefectibility' of the Church. In line with the teaching on this topic given in the two previous statements on *Authority in the Church,* *The Gift of Authority* bases its account of indefectibility on Christ's promise that his Spirit will lead his people into all truth:

> In every age Christians have said 'Amen' to Christ's promise that the Spirit will guide his Church into all truth. The New Testament frequently echoes this promise by referring to the boldness, assurance and certainty to which Christians can lay claim (cf. Lk 1.4; 1 Thess 2.2; Eph 3.2; Heb 11.1). In their concern to make the Gospel accessible to all who are open to receive it, those charged with the ministry of memory and teaching have accepted new and hitherto unfamiliar expressions of faith. Some of these formulations have initially generated doubt and disagreement about their fidelity to the apostolic Tradition. In the process of testing such formulations, the Church has moved cautiously, but with confidence in the promise of Christ that it will persevere and be maintained in the truth (cf. Mt 16.18; Jn 16.13). This is what is meant by the indefectibility of the Church.[16]

Having defined indefectibility in this way, *The Gift of Authority* then concludes that the fulfilment of Christ's promise means that the Church receives guidance from the Holy Spirit 'that keeps its teaching faithful to apostolic Tradition'.[17]

While the belief that Christ will uphold his Church and prevent it straying into apostasy is one that has been universally accepted in Christian theology and is therefore uncontroversial, the way that *The Gift of Authority* develops this idea is controversial for two reasons.

- Firstly, the term 'apostolic Tradition' is problematic because if it implies that there is tradition stemming from the apostles that is not contained in Scripture then many Christians would question whether any such tradition actually exists,[18] and if it means the apostolic Tradition contained in the New Testament then it would have been better to say that the guidance of the Spirit will keep the Church faithful to the teaching of the New Testament.

- Secondly, the argument that the indefectibility of the Church means that the Church will always be faithful to apostolic teaching not only runs counter to the Anglican tradition,[19] but is also contrary to the teaching of Scripture (see for example Galatians 1.6-7, 1 Timothy 4.1-3, 2 Peter 2.1-3, Revelation 2.12-29) and to the witness of Church history which indicates that the

Church has constantly fallen into error throughout its history. For instance, in the fourth century large parts of the Church embraced various kinds of Arianism, while in the last century large parts of the German Church gave support to Nazism.

It could be argued that the Church as a whole did not succumb to such errors and that whatever errors have afflicted particular parts of the Church have eventually been rejected by the Church as a whole. This may be true, but (a) those who have rejected these errors have invariably succumbed to errors of their own, and (b) whenever the Church has overcome one error then another one has inevitably cropped up. There has been no period in Church history where the Church has been free from what later generations have come to recognize as error.

The reason for this is twofold. It is because, as St Augustine argued on the basis of Matthew 13.47-50, the Church as a visible human institution always contains both good fish and bad, those who are truly committed to Christ and those who are not.[20] It is also because even those who do belong to Christ are not in this life fully perfect and free from sin, and are therefore always liable to err in matters concerning both faith and ethics. In the words of Article XV of the *Thirty-Nine Articles*, although Christ was perfect and without sin, 'all we the rest, although baptized and born again in Christ, yet offend in many things; and if we say we have no sin, we deceive ourselves, and the truth is not in us'.

The combination of the fact that there are those in the visible Church who are not truly Christians, and that even those who are are always liable to error because of the effects of sin, means that the maintenance of the Church by God is a matter of faith rather than sight. We cannot read the actions of God off the page of history and be assured that God is keeping his promise because the Church is at all times preserved from error. Our confidence has to rest in God and his fidelity, and in that alone.

4   the faith of the individual and the faith of the community

The fourth area that is problematic is what *The Gift of Authority* says about the assent of the individual believer to the faith of the community. Its statement that, 'The believer's "Amen" to Christ becomes yet more complete as that person receives all that the Church, in faithfulness to the Word of God, affirms to be the content of divine revelation'(12)[21] raises two difficulties.

The first difficulty is that in a context in which the Church of Christ is divided and in which different parts of the Church understand the content of divine revelation in different ways, some of which are, as we have already noted, contradictory, it is difficult to see what this statement would mean in practice. What does the term 'Church' refer to in this connection?

The second difficulty is the fact that the statement is ambiguous.

- It can be read as meaning that what the Church affirms to be the content of divine revelation will in fact be faithful to the Word of God. If this is what is meant then the question of the susceptibility of the Church to error arises again.
- On the other hand, it can be read as saying that the believer only has to receive what is in fact faithful to the Word of God. This second reading would be preferable in that it would protect that 'integrity of the believer's conscience' to which the text goes on to refer. However, what the text says about individual Christians being called to 'say "Amen" to all that the whole company of Christians receives and teaches as the authentic meaning of the Gospel and the way to follow Christ'[22] points us in the direction of the first reading and the problems that it raises.

It would be more just to say that Christians have a duty to take seriously and to learn from what other Christians living and dead have believed, but that they are only called on to affirm what they can conscientiously accept as in conformity to the Word of God, and have a duty to question inherited teaching when they believe that it does not so conform.

Karl Barth gets the balance right in his *Evangelical Theology* when he discusses the question of the relationship of theological enquiry to the faith of the community:

> fundamental trust instead of mistrust will be the initial attitude of theology towards the tradition which determines the present-day Church. And any questions and proposals which theology has to direct to the tradition will definitely not be forced on the community like a decree; any such findings will be presented only as well-weighed suggestions. Nevertheless, no ecclesiastical authority should be allowed by theology to hinder it from honestly pursuing its critical task, and the same applies to any frightened voices in the midst of the rest of the congregation. The task of theology is to discuss freely the reservations as well as the proposals for improvement which occur to it in reflection on the inherited witness of the community. Theology says *credo*,

I believe, along with the present day community and its fathers. But it says *credo ut intelligam*, 'I believe in order to understand.' To achieve this understanding it must be granted leeway for the good of the community itself.[23]

At its best the Anglican tradition has sought to uphold precisely this balance between respect for the inherited faith of the Christian community and freedom for responsible theological enquiry, and it is this balance which *The Gift of Authority*, in spite of all it says about respect for conscience and the importance of the work of theologians, seems to call into question.

5   the acceptance of episcopal authority

The fifth problem is the related area of the acceptance by the individual believer of the exercise of authority by their bishop. In its account of this subject *The Gift of Authority* claims that decisions taken by a bishop in performing their episcopal duties 'have an authority which the faithful have a duty to receive and accept' and that: 'By their *sensus fidei* the faithful are able in conscience both to recognise God at work in the bishop's exercise of authority, and also to respond to it as believers.'[24] This is a claim that raises a number of difficulties.

It is, of course, true that Christians have a general duty to obey those in authority in the Church. Hebrews 13.17 says explicitly, for example, 'Obey your leaders and submit to them.' However, the New Testament also declares that 'We must obey God rather than men' (Acts 5.29), and in any particular case where obedience is asked for both these principles have to be borne in mind.

Unless one assumes that what a bishop does is always in conformity with the will of God one has to be open to the possibility that a bishop may ask someone to do something that is contrary to God's will. If a believer holds that is in fact the case then they can have no alternative, out of loyalty to God, but to refuse to obey.

Church history provides numerous examples of such principled disobedience, and in refusing to recognize the issue *The Gift of Authority* fails to reflect the life of the Church as it actually is. It is simply not true that the faithful are always able in good conscience to recognize God at work in the actions of their bishops.

That is why the Church of England, for example, has never required that believers should always accept what their bishops are doing, and why the oath of canonical obedience in the Anglican ordinals is restricted to obedience in 'all things lawful and honest'. Absolute and unquestioning obedience is not called for.

Similarly, Roman Catholic Canon Law specifically envisages disobedience where the bishop himself is breaking the law of the Church.

What would be helpful is if ARCIC II could consider how the balance between proper respect for episcopal authority, and the right of the believer to dissent and to challenge what their bishop is doing, should be worked out in the life of the Church.

6   the teaching authority of bishops

The sixth area in which there are problems is what *The Gift of Authority* says about the teaching authority of bishops. There are five issues here, which require further discussion, and these are enumerated as points I–V below.

(I) Does The Gift of Authority do justice to the complex nature of the exercise of teaching authority within the Church?

The Gift of Authority paints a simple picture of a Church in which the faith of the people of God is articulated by the bishops in ways that the faithful then recognize as authentic.

Leaving aside for the moment the question of what happens if the faithful do not give this recognition, or are divided about whether this recognition should be given, the main question that needs to be asked about this picture is whether in fact the role of the bishops is as important in expressing the faith of the Church as *The Gift of Authority* suggests.

Could it not be argued that the work of non-episcopal clergy and lay people has been at least as important in expressing the faith in ways which have received recognition as authentic? One only has to mention names such as Justin Martyr, St Thomas Aquinas, Julian of Norwich, Martin Luther, and C. S. Lewis for this point to become obvious.

It is true *The Gift of Authority* acknowledges the responsibility of the whole people of God for 'the discernment, actualisation and communication of the word of God'. However, in giving a unique importance to the bishop's teaching role what it does not acknowledge is that authoritative teaching is not only given by bishops but equally by others as well, and that the work of these others is not necessarily recognized as authoritative because of episcopal endorsement.

In the history of the Church, the work of many ordained and lay Christians has been recognized as possessing intrinsic authority because of the powerful way in which it has borne witness to Christian truth, and such recognition has taken place with or without episcopal endorsement, and sometimes in the face of episcopal opposition.

Martin Luther is a classic example of this point. His work received intense opposition from the episcopal hierarchy of his day and yet it has come to be seen by most Christians (Roman Catholics included) as bearing authoritative witness to important facets of Christian truth.

Another dimension of this issue, one that has become increasingly important in both the Anglican Communion and the Roman Catholic Church since the 1960s, is the authority of prophetic sayings believed to be uttered under the direct guidance of the Spirit.

Many in both traditions would see such prophetic words as possessing direct God-given authority, and in the nature of the case this authority would be separate and distinct from official episcopal teaching. A related issue in the Roman Catholic Church would be the status of teachings given as a result of visions, such as the vision of the Blessed Virgin Mary said to have been seen at Fatima.

These kinds of prophetic words and visions are very controversial, but they are important in the life of the Church and it would be irresponsible simply to ignore them.

What all this means is that the exercise and recognition of authoritative teaching within the Church is a complex rather than a simple matter, and what is lacking in *The Gift of Authority* is a proper recognition of this complexity and how the different forms of authoritative teaching that exist in the Church should relate to one another.

It is clearly the case, as the Church of England's Ordinals and Canon Law emphasize,[25] that in an episcopally ordered Church the bishops have a particular responsibility to ensure that the teaching given in and by the Church remains faithful to the Gospel, and that they themselves have an important teaching ministry.

However, this does not mean, as *The Gift of Authority* seems to suggest, that the bishops have a uniquely authoritative teaching authority to the extent that they alone can and do articulate teaching to which the faithful are called to say 'Amen'.

(II) Does The Gift of Authority *do justice to the importance of the synodical dimension of the Anglican system of Church government?*

The Gift of Authority declares that it is the bishops who are 'to determine what is to be taught as faithful to the apostolic Tradition'.[26] This may be a true reflection of the position in the Roman Catholic Church, but it certainly does not reflect the position within the Anglican tradition.

As *The Gift of Authority* notes, 'Houses of Bishops exercise a distinctive and unique ministry in relation to matters of doctrine, worship and moral life'.[27] This is true in the Anglican Communion as it is in the Roman Catholic Church. However, in the Anglican tradition this ministry is exercised with the agreement of, and in consultation with, the representatives of the clergy and the laity. Episcopal teaching only becomes the official teaching of the Church of England when it has the consent of the clergy and laity explicitly given by their duly appointed representatives.

What the Church of England, for example, believes and teaches concerning doctrine, worship and the moral life is determined not by the bishops alone but also by the clerical and lay members of General Synod with the additional agreement of Parliament in certain circumstances. With the exception of the involvement of Parliament, a similar situation also exists in the other provinces of the Anglican Communion.

Furthermore, it is certainly not the case that the clerical and lay representatives in Anglican synods simply give assent to what the bishops have decided. They have both a right and a duty to criticize and even to reject what the bishops suggest if they believe it to be wrong.

This right and duty of clergy and laity to scrutinize, affirm, challenge or, in the last resort, reject episcopal teaching is one of the major differences between the Anglican and Roman Catholic traditions, and it is one that *The Gift of Authority* does not accurately reflect.

As the American Anglican Ronald Young puts it: 'The examples illustrating Anglican synodality emphasize the dominant power of the bishop. They ignore the complementary and mutual authority exercised by the three orders of episcopate, clergy and laity in the church's primary governing institutions.'[28] One might question Young's use of the term 'order' to refer to the 'laity', since the laity are not a distinct order within the Church, but the basic criticism he makes of *The Gift of Authority* is nonetheless valid.

The Gift of Authority notes that among the challenges facing Roman Catholics is the need to ensure effective participation of the clergy and laity in the Church's synodical structures, and the need to ensure that a variety of theological opinion is taken into account when decisions are made about the life of the Church. It is by sharing the distinctive strengths of their own synodical structures that Anglicans can best help Roman Catholics to face these challenges.

It is also true, however, that the Anglican synodical model is not perfect, and that Anglicans, in turn, need to give attention to a eucharistic model for synods in which emphasis is laid on reaching a common mind. This emphasis would counteract the major weakness of the present Anglican model which is that proceeding on the basis of majority voting can lead to the exclusion or marginalization of those holding a minority viewpoint. A eucharistic model in which emphasis is laid on the importance of everyone present being able to utter an 'Amen' to what has been decided, provides an important counterbalance to the current Anglican tendency to think in terms of winners and losers in synodical debates.

What is required is for both the 'eucharistic' and 'parliamentary' models to be employed in creative tension as valid ways of highlighting different aspects of how synods should operate in such a way as to enable God's people to hear his voice and seek to obey it together.

(III) Does The Gift of Authority *give a convincing explanation of the relationship between the authority of episcopal teaching and its reception by the faithful?*

Chapter III of *The Gift of Authority* declares that:

> The duty of maintaining the Church in the truth is one of the essential functions of the episcopal college. It has the power to exercise this ministry because it is bound in succession to the apostles, who were the body authorised and sent by Christ to preach the Gospel to all the nations.[29]

And that:

> In specific circumstances, those with this ministry of oversight (*episcope*), assisted by the Holy Spirit, may together come to a judgement which, being faithful to Scripture and consistent with apostolic Tradition, is preserved from error. By such a judgement, which is a renewed expression of God's one 'Yes' in Jesus Christ, the Church is maintained in truth so that it may continue to offer its 'Amen' to the glory of God. This is what is meant when it is affirmed that the Church may teach *infallibly*.[30]

Although the chapter thus emphasizes the teaching authority of the bishops, it also insists that the people of God as a whole are involved in the exercise of teaching authority in the Church. As the chapter puts it, 'reception of teaching is integral to the process'. What enables the Church to say 'Amen' to authoritative teaching put forward by the bishops is the recognition by the whole people of God that, 'this teaching expresses the apostolic faith and operates within the authority and truth of Christ, the Head of the Church'.[31]

In support of this claim the chapter then refers in a footnote to the teaching of the Second Vatican Council:

> The whole body of the faithful who have an anointing that comes from the holy one (cf. 1 Jn 2.20, 2.27) cannot err in matters of belief. This characteristic is shown in the supernatural appreciation of the faith (*sensus fidei*) of the whole people, when, 'from the bishops to the last of the faithful' they manifest a universal consent in matters of faith and morals' (Dogmatic Constitution on the Church, *Lumen Gentium*, 12).[32]

There are four questions that need to be addressed to this argument.

- Firstly, what are the specific circumstances in which such infallible teaching may be given? No explanation is offered as to what these circumstances might be and no examples are given of occasions in the past where these circumstances existed and infallible teaching was duly given.
- Secondly, why is the infallible teaching of the Church exclusively identified with the teaching given by bishops? As has been argued earlier in this chapter, in actual fact authoritative teaching is not exclusively given by bishops alone, but by clergy and laity as well, and, indeed, by the whole people of God taking counsel together. Might not this teaching also be described as 'infallible' in the sense of being preserved from error?
- Thirdly, is the picture of reception given here a realistic one? It is easy to write about the 'universal consent' of the people of God,

but in reality it is difficult, if not impossible, to discover what every person within a particular church thinks about a doctrinal definition let alone what the consensus of all God's people in all the different churches actually is, even assuming that they have heard of the doctrinal definition in question.

Furthermore, in the history of the Church there has rarely, if ever, been complete and permanent unanimity about whether or not a particular doctrinal formulation is correct. What has happened is that over a long period of time a particular viewpoint has come to prevail and has been generally accepted, although some people may continue to disagree, and the issue at stake may be reopened for general discussion at some point in the future.

- Fourthly, does not the recognition that doctrinal definitions have been disputed, plus the recognition that the Church and its members are always liable to error, mean that the fact that a doctrinal definition has been generally received is not in itself a guarantee of its truth? After all, as Bishop John Jewel pointed out back in the sixteenth century, a minority can often be in the right, and conversely, unanimity is not a guarantee of truth. As he says, there was perfect unanimity among the Israelites who worshipped the golden calf and those in the crowd in Jerusalem who called for the crucifixion of Our Lord.

In the end, the question is surely not whether a definition has been widely received but whether it is true. In deciding this question Christians must take extremely seriously the considered opinion of the other members of the body of Christ, but in the last resort each individual Christian has the responsibility before God of testing what is proposed against the canon of Scripture and seeing if the two correspond.

The fundamental question here is the right of the individual Christian to exercise his or her private judgement in matters of Christian belief, a matter which has already been touched on in connection with the issues of the freedom of theological enquiry, and the duty of the faithful to obey their bishops.

On the one hand, it would be wrong for an individual Christian to ignore the *sensus fidelium* without a very good reason for doing so. As the 1938 report *Doctrine in the Church of England* puts it:

> All Christians are bound to allow very high authority to doctrines which the Church has been generally united in teaching; for each believer has a limited range, and the basis of the Church's faith is far wider than that of his own can ever be.

> An individual Christian who rejects any part of that belief is guilty
> of presumption, unless he feels himself bound in conscience
> to do so and has substantial reasons for holding that what
> he rejects is not essential to the truth and value
> of Christianity.[33]

On the other hand, it also remains true that, as the Anglican
theologian W. H. Griffith Thomas puts it: 'The last and final authority
must be the Word of God illuminating, influencing and controlling the
human conscience and reason through the presence and power of
the Spirit of God.'[34] As he says, this position:

> is that which is the most consonant with the nature of our
> personality and its responsibility to God. It is the assertion of
> our indefeasible right to be in direct personal relationship to God,
> while welcoming all possible light from every quarter as helping
> us to decide for ourselves under the guidance of God's Word
> and Spirit.[35]

It is true that The Gift of Authority urges respect for the individual
conscience: 'because the divine work of salvation affirms human
freedom'.[36] However, its great emphasis on the faith of the Christian
community as the place where theological truth is to be found fails to
do proper justice to the fact that the final authority for each individual
has to be their own perception of the truth of God, and to the fact
that they have a duty to be loyal to this truth whatever the Christian
community as a whole decides.

(IV) Does The Gift of Authority make too exclusive an identification between apostolicity and episcopal ministry?

The Gift of Authority argues that the episcopal college has a special
responsibility for maintaining the Church in truth because 'it is bound
in succession to the apostles, who were the body authorised and
sent by Christ to preach the Gospel to all the nations'.[37] This
statement seems to identify apostolicity and episcopal ministry in
an exclusive fashion whereas recent ecumenical thinking, which the
Church of England and other branches of the Anglican Communion
have endorsed, has seen apostolicity as an attribute of the Church
as a whole.

For example, The Porvoo Common Statement, issued in 1993 by
the British and Irish Anglican Churches and the Nordic and Baltic
Lutheran Churches, declares that the apostolic mandate to preach
the Gospel is given to the Church as a whole:

The Church today is charged, as were the apostles, to proclaim the gospel to all nations, because the good news about Jesus Christ is the disclosure of God's eternal plan for the reconciliation of all things in his Son. The Church is called to faithfulness to the normative apostolic witness to the life, death and resurrection of its Lord. The Church receives its mission and the power to fulfil its mission as a gift of the risen Christ. The Church is thus apostolic as whole. 'Apostolicity means that the Church is sent by Jesus to be for the world, to participate in his mission and therefore in the mission of the One who sent Jesus, to participate in the mission of the Father and the Son through the dynamic of the Holy Spirit.'[38]

According to the *Porvoo* statement the existence of the episcopal office serves to highlight the apostolic nature of the Church as a whole.

The ultimate ground of the fidelity of the Church, in continuity with the apostles, is the promise of the Lord and the presence of the Holy Spirit at work in the whole Church. The continuity of the ministry of oversight is to be understood within the continuity of the apostolic life and mission of the whole Church. Apostolic succession in the episcopal office is a visible and personal way of focusing the apostolicity of the whole Church.[39]

To put it simply, the difference between *The Gift of Authority* and the ecumenical thinking reflected in the Porvoo statement is that the former seems to see the college of bishops as the possessors of the apostolic commission whereas the latter sees this commission as given to the Church as a whole, and the existence of bishops in historic succession as witnessing to this fact.

Given that the Church of England and other branches of the Anglican Communion have officially accepted statements that express the latter viewpoint, the tension between this viewpoint and what is said in *The Gift of Authority* will need to be resolved.

(V) Is The Gift of Authority right to tie together the authenticity of episcopal teaching with the unanimity of the episcopal college?

The last point that needs to be raised in connection with what is said about the authority of episcopal teaching concerns the statement that: 'The authenticity of the teaching of individual bishops is evident when this teaching is in solidarity with that of the whole episcopal college.'[40]

What we have here once again is an example of the tendency of *The Gift of Authority* to equate unanimity and truth. The logic of *The Gift of Authority*'s own emphasis on the primacy of Scripture would seem to point in a different direction.

It would be better to say that while a unanimous decision by the whole episcopal college does carry considerable moral authority, nevertheless the authenticity of this decision depends on its conformity with Scripture. This would mean that a dissenting opinion that is in conformity with Scripture is more 'authentic' than a majority opinion that is not.

7   papal primacy

The seventh area of *The Gift of Authority* in which problems remain is what is said about the subject of papal primacy.

As the House of Bishops' paper *May They All Be One* explains, the notion of universal primacy is not in itself impossible for Anglicans to accept:

> Anglicans are . . . by no means opposed to the principle and practice of a personal ministry at the world level in the service of unity. Indeed, increasingly their experience of the Anglican Communion is leading them to appreciate the proper need, alongside communal and collegial ministries, for a personal service of unity in the faith.[41]

Furthermore, because the argument for papal primacy developed in *The Gift of Authority* is in fact simply a restatement of what is said about this subject in the two previous ARCIC statements on authority, and because what was said there received general acceptance both from the 1988 Lambeth Conference and the Church of England House of Bishops, it might be argued that Anglicans should accept what is said in *The Gift of Authority* as well.

However, it is not possible to take this approach because, notwithstanding this earlier agreement, the way in which the argument for a universal papal primacy is developed in *The Gift of Authority* raises a number of serious problems which will need to be tackled if there is to be further progress in this area.

The first problem relates to the argument that is offered for accepting papal primacy. Building on the arguments for papal primacy offered in the two previous ARCIC statements on authority, *The Gift of Authority* seems to offer a combined theological and historical case for the papal office.

First, it is argued that a primatial ministry is required by the Church as a whole: 'The exigencies of church life call for a specific exercise of *episcope* at the service of the whole Church.'[42]

Second, it is argued that Peter exercised such a ministry in the early Church: 'In the pattern found in the New Testament one of the twelve is chosen by Jesus Christ to strengthen the others so that they will remain faithful to their mission and in harmony with each other.'

And third, it is then noted that the Bishop of Rome has historically exercised such a ministry for the benefit of the whole Church:

> Historically, the Bishop of Rome has exercised such a ministry either for the benefit of the whole Church, as when Leo contributed to the Council of Chalcedon, or for the benefit of a local church, as when Gregory the Great supported Augustine of Canterbury's mission and ordering of the English church.[43]

The logic of the argument seems to be that a Petrine type of primacy is required in the Church; historically the Pope has fulfilled this role, so therefore papal primacy should be accepted by the Church.

Possibly because an acceptance of the argument in the previous ARCIC statements on authority is assumed, what is missing here is any engagement with the arguments of those who would question each part of this argument.

- There is no engagement with those who think that a universal primacy with authority over the local or national church is unnecessary and would necessarily lead to the curtailment of the right of the local or national church to make its own decisions before God.
- There is no engagement with those who would say that while St Peter did exercise a leadership role in the Early Church, there is no evidence that he exercised any kind of authority over the other apostles or that he had a unique role in expressing or formulating the faith of the Church that was different from that of other apostles such as St John or St Paul.
- There is no engagement with those who would say that the argument that the Bishop of Rome has exercised authority 'for the benefit of the whole Church' depends on a very selective reading of papal history, and that the negative aspects of that history point to the conclusion that overall the exercise of papal primacy has done the Church more harm than good.

Responses can be made to each of these arguments, but *The Gift of Authority* fails to make them and so it appears to be skating over the problems relating to papal primacy rather than tackling them.

It also seems to skate over the problem of the relationship between its understanding of the relationship between the ministry given to St Peter and the subsequent ministry of the Bishop of Rome, and the account of this relationship given at the First Vatican Council in 1870 in its *Dogmatic Constitution of the Church of Christ*.

The approach taken in *Authority in the Church I & II* to which *The Gift of Authority* refers is that there is an analogy rather than a direct historical continuity between the ministry exercised by St Peter and the ministry subsequently exercised by the Bishop of Rome. The furthest it goes is to suggest that:

> it is possible to think that a primacy of the bishop of Rome is not contrary to the New Testament and is part of God's purpose regarding the Church's unity and catholicity, while admitting that the New Testament texts offer no sufficient basis for this.[44]

The Dogmatic Constitution, on the other hand, teaches that: 'according to the testimony of the Gospel, the primacy of jurisdiction over the universal Church of God was immediately and directly promised and given to the Blessed Peter the Apostle by Christ the Lord', and that:

> whosoever succeeds to Peter in this See, does by the institution of Christ Himself obtain the Primacy of Peter over the whole Church. The disposition made by the Incarnate Truth therefore remains, and Blessed Peter, abiding through the strength of the Rock in the power that he received, has not abandoned the direction of the Church.[45]

In its official response to ARCIC I the Vatican identified the divergence between these two approaches as an issue that required further attention. *The Gift of Authority*, however, has failed to address it.

This is an issue that is important not only to the Vatican but also to Anglicans as well, since many Anglicans who might be willing to accept that the ministry of St Peter provides a model for a universal primacy in the Church would be unable to accept the argument of *Vatican I* that the papal office was directly given to St Peter and his successors by Christ himself.

The second problem raised by what *The Gift of Authority* says about papal primacy relates to the statement that when the Bishop of

Rome utters a solemn definition from the chair of Peter, what he utters is 'the wholly reliable teaching of the whole Church'.[46] There are four difficulties with this statement.

- Is there any Scriptural or theological justification for thinking that when making such a pronouncement the Bishop of Rome is in fact preserved from error?
- In the absence of such preservation, how can we be sure that what he declares is actually the faith of the whole Church, given the fact that *The Gift of Authority* acknowledges that human weakness and sin affect the Bishop of Rome just as much as everyone else?
- What is the evidence that in actual fact such solemn definitions have expressed the faith of the *whole* Church? Many Christians, including most Anglicans, would say, for example, that the solemn definitions made regarding the immaculate conception and bodily assumption of the Blessed Virgin Mary certainly do not reflect what they believe.
- Even the argument that the authority being assigned to the Pope is no greater than the authority generally given to the decisions of ecumenical councils is problematic, given that Article XXI of the *Thirty-Nine Articles* declares explicitly that General Councils of the Church 'may err, and sometimes have erred, even in things pertaining unto God'.[47]

It has been suggested that what is being described here is an ideal primacy exercised in a reunited Church, but (a) the language that is used in this section of *The Gift of Authority* simply does not permit such an interpretation,[48] and (b) even if this were the case, the four issues just identified would remain to be tackled.

The third problem raised by what *The Gift of Authority* says about papal primacy is that of how far the Roman Catholic Church would be prepared to take the principle that there may be a need for 'loyal criticism and reforms' of the Papacy.[49]

In his encyclical *Ut Unum Sint*, to which *The Gift of Authority* refers, Pope John Paul II has invited the leaders and theologians of other Churches to engage in a 'patient and fraternal dialogue' about the exercise of the papal office. The question is what the outcome of this dialogue might be. Can we envisage a situation where the exercise of papal ministry was fundamentally different from what it is today because the ideas and concerns of other Churches have been noted and then responded to?

Furthermore, would a willingness to accept criticism mean a willingness to accept that previous Bishops of Rome may have erred in the exercise of their ministries and that therefore it may be legitimate to revisit past papal pronouncements such as the Marian dogmas mentioned above or the condemnation of Anglican orders in *Apostolicae Curae* to see whether they were correct?

The fourth problem raised by what *The Gift of Authority* says about papal primacy is what it fails to say about the claim traditionally made by the Bishop of Rome for immediate and ordinary jurisdiction over all churches and their bishops. This is a claim that Anglicans have rejected since the sixteenth century because they have felt that it fails to respect the legitimate authority belonging to other bishops and the legitimate freedom of the local church to manage its own affairs and, where necessary, to reform itself under the word of God.

The two previous ARCIC reports on *Authority in the Church* both considered this issue, but as the FOAG response to ARCIC I noted, it is still a matter that causes Anglicans concern:

> It is one thing to acknowledge the personal primacy of the bishop of Rome, together with his duty to intervene when the unity of Christian communion is in peril. It is another thing to accept the degree of centralization of Church government which still appears to be associated with it. Anglicans could not be happy with an interpretation of jurisdiction which saw the proper autonomy of local bishops and churches as a matter of delegation or concession from central authority, rather than as a matter of inherent right.[50]

The same concern is also raised in *May They All Be One* which, while arguing that a universal primacy must have both 'doctrinal and disciplinary elements', nevertheless declares that:

> In matters of discipline and the oversight of the communion of the Church we should not minimize the serious obstacles that still exist because of the present Roman Catholic understanding of the jurisdiction attributed to the primacy of the Bishop of Rome. The claim that the Bishop of Rome has by divine institution ordinary, immediate and universal jurisdiction over the whole Church is seen by some as a threat to the integrity of the episcopal college and to the apostolic authority of the bishops, those brothers Peter was commanded to strengthen.[51]

The Gift of Authority only touches on this issue obliquely in the questions addressed to Roman Catholics at the end of the statement. Such an oblique reference is insufficient when this is such a critical issue. What is required is a substantive and critical discussion, which looks directly at the teaching given on this issue both in Chapter 3 of the *Dogmatic Constitution on the Church* and, more recently, in section 22 of *Lumen Gentium*.

The *Dogmatic Constitution* declares that:

> by divine ordinance the Roman Church possesses a pre-eminence of ordinary power over every other church, and . . . this jurisdictional power of the Roman Pontiff is both episcopal and immediate. Both clergy and faithful of whatever rite and dignity both singly and collectively, are bound to submit to this power by the duty of hierarchical subordination and true obedience, and this not only in matters concerning faith and morals, but also in those which regard the discipline and government of the Church throughout the world.

And *Lumen Gentium*, while emphasizing the importance of the college of bishops as a whole, nonetheless states unequivocally that:

> the college or body of bishops has no authority unless it is simultaneously conceived of in terms of its head, the Roman Pontiff, Peter's successor and without any lessening of his power of primacy over all, pastors as well as the general faithful. For in virtue of his office, that is, as Vicar of Christ and pastor of the whole Church, the Roman Pontiff has full, supreme, and universal power over the Church. And he can always exercise this power freely.

These statements are never referred to in *The Gift of Authority* and this is a major omission since, for the reasons given above, the view of the Papacy which they contain is a major obstacle to an Anglican acceptance of papal primacy. If the Anglican Communion and the Roman Catholic Church are ever to reach agreement on the role of the Papacy, the issues raised by these statements will have to be dealt with.

8   the reception of papal primacy

The eighth and final area in which problems remain is the proposal at the end of the statement that Anglicans should be prepared to receive the gift of papal primacy prior to the establishment of full communion between the Anglican Communion and the Roman Catholic Church.

Many Anglicans will warm to the attractive sketch of the characteristics of a renewed universal primacy in paragraph 61 of *The Gift of Authority*, which we noted at the beginning of this chapter. However, the statement in paragraph 60, 'The Commission's work has resulted in sufficient agreement on universal primacy as a gift to be shared, for us to propose that such a primacy could be offered and received even before our churches are in full communion',[52] would raise grave difficulties for those Anglicans who still have objections to the idea of a universal papal primacy as such. Their objections would need to be considered and overcome before such a move would be feasible.

Furthermore, even those Anglicans who would be happy with such a primacy in principle are likely to want to know more about what this would mean in practice.

There are a number of important issues which Anglicans and Roman Catholics still need to explore together. What difference would it actually make to the way that Anglicanism operates to accept papal primacy? Precisely what aspects of papal authority and jurisdiction would Anglicans be asked to accept? What would happen if Anglicans wished to take a line of action of which the Pope disapproved? Would they still be free to do so?

The acceptance of papal primacy by the Anglican Communion is only ever likely to take place if Anglicans and Roman Catholics can reach agreement on the answers to these questions.

conclusion

From an Anglican standpoint there is much that is helpful about *The Gift of Authority*, and to which we can say 'Amen'. It represents a clear growth in agreement between the Anglican and Roman Catholic traditions in a number of very important areas of theology over which they have previously been divided.

However, the word 'No' also has to be said because the statement as a whole is problematic for three main reasons.

1. The statement is insufficiently realistic about the history and present life of the Church. It does not deal with problems raised by the study of Church history for the theological claims it makes about the preservation of the Church from error and the unity of faith brought about by the exercise of the *sensus fidelium*. It also does not do justice to the reality of disagreement and conflict in the life of the Church, and to the fact that the many and varied forms of authority that exist in the Church cannot be reduced

to a simple formula of bishops expressing the faith of the whole people of God in a way that they then universally recognize and accept.

2. The statement does not give sufficient recognition to the importance of minority opinion, conscientious dissent, and the inalienable right and duty of the individual believer to exercise their own private theological judgement in submission to the word of God in Scripture.

   The Gift of Authority lays great emphasis on the importance of consensus as a guide to truth, but what it does not acknowledge is that, in a fallen world and in a Church which is still only on the way to the attainment of the full vision of God, consensus is not an infallible guide because there can be consensus in error as well as in truth. In this situation, dissenting voices have to be attended to because they can represent the voice of God, and in the last resort each individual has to make their own decision about truth and cannot pass the responsibility on to anyone else.

3. The statement leaves unresolved and undiscussed a number of important issues to do with the origins and exercise of papal authority. These issues, such as the negative aspects of papal history, the theological status of solemn papal definitions, and the papal claim to immediate, ordinary, universal jurisdiction, will need to be tackled before an Anglican acceptance of papal primacy ever becomes a realistic prospect.

There therefore needs to be further discussion that complements and clarifies what is said in *The Gift of Authority* by means of a serious exploration of issues to do with the place of dissent, disagreement and conflict in the Church, and the nature and extent of papal authority.

chapter four

an ecumenical
hermeneutic of trust

Christopher Hill

introduction

The responses to *The Gift of Authority* have been extraordinarily varied. From time to time one would think that different critics were reading an entirely different text. This may indicate a certain amount of eisegesis as well as exegesis; that is to say there is as much interpretation being *put into* the text as being *read out* of it. We all come to texts with certain presuppositions and assumptions, and *The Gift of Authority* is certainly no exception to this. A factor that has surprised me on reading some of the more negative criticisms of *The Gift of Authority* is that it has not been read in the context of earlier Anglican/Roman Catholic discussions. This in spite of the fact that the text of *The Gift of Authority* specifically claims that it does not start from nothing but builds upon the work of the first Anglican–Roman Catholic Commission and its earlier statements on authority (*Authority I* and *II* and their *Elucidations*).[1]

The Anglican–Roman Catholic International Commission explicitly records the formal degree of acceptance given to the earlier work on authority at the Lambeth Conference of 1988. It is worthwhile quoting the relevant Resolution of Lambeth 1988 in full, as well as the Note attached to it. The Conference:

> Welcomes *Authority in the Church (I and II)* together with the *Elucidation*, as a firm basis for the direction and agenda of the continuing dialogue on authority and wishes to encourage ARCIC II to continue to explore the basis in Scripture and tradition of the concept of a universal primacy, in conjunction with collegiality, as an instrument of unity, the character of such a primacy in practice, and to draw upon the experience of other Christian Churches in exercising primacy, collegiality and conciliarity. (Resolution 8.3)

To this a note was attached as follows:

The responses from the Provinces to the two Statements on Authority in the Church were generally positive. Questions were, however, raised about a number of matters, especially primacy, jurisdiction and infallibility, collegiality, and the role of the laity. Nevertheless, it was generally felt that *Authority in the Church* (I and II), together with the *Elucidation*, give us real grounds for believing that fuller agreement can be reached, and that they set out helpfully the direction and agenda of the way forward.

Crucially, *The Gift of Authority* accepts the decision of the Lambeth Conference that the general direction set in *Authority I* and *II* of the earlier Anglican–Roman Catholic International Commission was 'a firm basis for the direction and agenda of the continuing dialogue'.

Ecumenical memory can sometimes be short. It is worthwhile recalling that the discussion about the earlier ARCIC work on authority at the Lambeth Conference 1988 was very carefully prepared and included discussion of synodical responses to the work of ARCIC I from all over the world. This was done in conjunction with the Lima Text of the Faith and Order Commission of the World Council of Churches, *Baptism, Eucharist* and *Ministry*. Never before had ecumenical texts been given such a rigorous and systematic examination throughout the worldwide Anglican Communion and a volume of analysis of these two ecumenical texts was published in preparation for the Lambeth Conference entitled *The Emmaus Report: A Report of the Anglican Ecumenical Consultation 1987*. This was published for the Anglican Consultative Council and circulated to the Anglican Communion and to every bishop before the 1988 Conference.[2] Nor was the debate a hole-in-the-corner affair at the Conference itself. A small but articulate group of bishops led by the Archbishop of Sydney proposed a substantially wrecking motion to the draft resolution of moderate acceptance. It was the Bishop of Bath and Wells, Dr George Carey himself, who led for the defence of the proposed resolution of qualified acceptance of the ARCIC material, which was eventually passed overwhelmingly. This is the background to the work of ARCIC III, which recapitulated the earlier work, summarizing it as follows:

- acknowledgement that the Spirit of the Risen Lord maintains the people of God in obedience to the Father's will. By this action of the Holy Spirit, the authority of the Lord is active in the Church (cf. *The Final Report, Authority in the Church I, 3*);
- a recognition that because of their baptism and their participation in the *sensus fidelium*, the laity play an integral part in decision-making in the Church (cf. *Authority in the Church: Elucidation*, 4);

- the complementarity of primacy and conciliarity as elements of *episcope* within the Church (cf. Authority in the Church I, 22);
- the need for a universal primacy exercised by the Bishop of Rome as a sign and safeguard of unity within a reunited Church (cf. *Authority in the Church II*, 9);
- the need for a universal primate to exercise his ministry in collegial association with the other bishops (cf. *Authority in the Church II*, 19);
- an understanding of universal primacy and conciliarity which complements and does not supplant the exercise of *episcope* in local churches (cf. *Authority in the Church I*, 21-23; *Authority in the Church II*, 19).[3]

The Gift of Authority raises interesting questions about ecumenical method. Is the ecumenical task solely that of a static examination of ecumenical documents against the light of historical confessional documents such as *The Thirty-Nine Articles* or *The Book of Common Prayer*? Are questions of authority badges of the continuity of separated Churches? Put crudely, is the cry of 'No Popery' more a question of Protestant identity than a serious discussion about authority in the Church?

Or, from a very different perspective, should discussions about authority only begin with modern or postmodern assumptions about the dissolution of the authority of office or text as such in today's (Western) cultures? The Lambeth Conference (1988) rejected the 'confessional' approach to ecumenical method, while encouraging a continued discussion on the basis that questions of authority could still be discussed in relation to Scripture, Tradition and the Community of the Church. This was the mandate ARCIC was given; however difficult the (post) modern discussion of authority has now become.

The Gift of Authority raises the question as to whether or not matters of authority can be received as gifts from other Christian traditions. This is a novel way of thinking about questions of authority and it should surely not be dismissed out of hand. To illustrate this, could not the Anglican tradition of synodical government, which integrally relates laity and clergy with bishops in the decision-making processes of the Church, be a gift to the Roman Catholic Church which heretofore has related authority questions more exclusively to the episcopate, or more usually the Papacy itself and its less than transparent structures? Equally, could a universal primacy in a renewed communion between Anglicans and Roman Catholics, as well as other Christians, have something to offer the universal

Church as a ministry of unity and discernment? *The Gift of Authority* cites the *Virginia Report* which itself examines Anglican attitudes and structures of authority within the Communion. These issues are highly relevant to a continuing debate about the nature of communion within the Anglican Communion. How is authority to be exercised at a wider level than a national Church? Is provincial autonomy (for which read provincial independence) a necessarily Christian approach to authority? What minimum structures should exist in a global communion at a global level? All these matters are raised for discussion in the *Virginia Report* and the present Pope himself has raised questions about his own ministry in his encyclical *Ut Unum Sint*, similarly cited by *The Gift of Authority*.

A final preliminary remark of ARCIC must be noted. It is the double affirmation that any structure of authority can be oppressive and destructive as opposed to the way of Jesus Christ. This is clearly recognized in *The Gift of Authority* (3)[3]. But equally, *The Gift of Authority* wrestles with the realistic recognition that structures of authority are indeed necessary in the Church and have always existed. It is easy to have a romantic assumption that power cannot be abused in more democratic-looking structures or in churches where the words power and authority are eschewed altogether. A house church can embody more oppressive structures of authority than the Papacy or Anglican diocesan episcopacy. All structures can be corrupted and indeed have been.

authority in the Church

Throughout *The Gift of Authority* we meet a dynamic understanding of the question rather than something fixed and static. In spite of a number of criticisms to the effect that the laity are excluded from an exercise of authority in *The Gift of Authority*, this seems hardly to correspond with the actual text of what is said in the document. Such criticisms rightly reflect perceptions about the present exercise of authority within the Roman Catholic Church. In ARCIC's dynamic understanding of authority the exercise and acceptance of authority in the Church 'is inseparable from the response of believers to the Gospel'. This leads on to the *leitmotif* of *The Gift of Authority*: God's 'Yes' and our 'Amen'. Authority is seen here as *personal, relational, dynamic, spiritual* and *intrinsic to faith* (7–10). If commentators ignore these crucial paragraphs they will misunderstand all that follows. It is claimed to be 'the key to the exposition of authority in this statement'. The corollary to this is that those exercises of oppressive authority in any church (which are not God's 'Yes' accepted in the freedom of our 'Amen') are *not* in accordance with Christ or the tenor of this agreement. For example, a Roman Catholic taking seriously this dynamic understanding of authority, God's 'Yes' and our 'Amen' – that is the integral relationship between the exercise of authority and the response of the whole church – should question whether a decision about, say, the marriage of clergy or the restriction of ordination to males, is an authentic exercise of authority because it lacks the 'Amen' of many people within that church.

But some Anglicans have read this dynamic understanding of God's 'Yes' and our 'Amen' as indicating a rather traditional Roman Catholic ecclesiology in which there is a strict division between the clergy and laity, especially the bishops and the rest of the church, according to which the hierarchy alone teaches and speaks, it being the duty of the laity to accept whatever is taught with docility. This is contradicted by *The Gift of Authority*'s insistence that the laity are *integrally* associated with decision-making in the Church. Nor does it reflect *The Gift of Authority*'s insistence on authority being personal, relational and intrinsic to faith. Nor would such a traditionalist understanding of authority be consistent with St Paul's Second Letter to the Corinthians which is where ARCIC draws its hermeneutic from. At 2 Corinthians 1.18-20 Paul speaks of the 'Yes' of God to humankind which will never fail to elicit an 'Amen' because all God's promises are confirmed in his 'Yes' to Christ. Elsewhere, Paul speaks of the Spirit of God speaking within us, articulating that which we cannot by ourselves express. Paul sees the same Spirit as active in his own exercise of authority in relation to the Corinthian church and in the Corinthian response for which he looks. In spite of difficulties he does not doubt that God is working through him and each faithful Christian at Corinth. This is the presumption of *The Gift of Authority* in making God's 'Yes' and our 'Amen' its *leitmotif*. Authority is always a double process, critical reception while not adding to the 'formal' authority of an initial decision confirms its authenticity or otherwise. The 'Yes/Amen' *leitmotif* is therefore both important and subtle. If something is not God's 'Yes' in Christ we are not intended to say 'Amen', for both come from the same Spirit and only if something is truly God's 'Yes' does the Spirit also call for our 'Amen'.

Individual and corporate faith and response are expounded carefully in *The Gift of Authority* (11–13). The role of individual conscience is accorded 'a vital part to play' but the believer's 'Amen' is 'to all that the whole company of Christians receive and teaches as the authentic meaning of the Gospel and the way to follow Christ'. Protestant individualism (not itself *classically* Protestant but post-

Enlightenment) is ruled out. So also would forms of individualistic liberalism or 'romantic' Anglo-Catholicism.

Authority is reflected in the whole Christian community, laity as well as clergy, bishops and Pope. 'The revealed Word, to which the apostolic community originally bore witness, is received and communicated *through the life of the whole* Christian community' (emphasis mine, 14). We here meet Tradition, *paradosis*: a dynamic concept as it finds expression in the Greek New Testament. This New Testament dynamic of *paradosis* is weakly served by the inevitable but static translation as 'tradition'. Nor is Tradition as *paradosis* understood as essentially intellectual or propositional. Tradition is the constitutive elements of ecclesial life. *The Gift of Authority* carefully defines its terminological use of this phrase. There is a 'constant and perpetual reception and communication of the revealed Word'. Our 'Amen' 'is a fruit of the Spirit who constantly guides the disciples into all truth; that is, into Christ who is the way, the truth and the life'(16). All this is part of the living *memory* of the Church. The notion of Tradition (better the dynamic *paradosis*; the life, teaching and practice of the apostolic Church being handed on) as a living corporate memory will be new to some Anglicans. It is, however, entirely consistent with the biblical notion of the 'story' of God's people handed on, most especially the crucial Passover paradigm in which the youngest person present receives the story of salvation and enters into it for himself. It is also at one with much contemporary NT hermeneutic, in which the stories about Jesus the Christ are re-told – handed on – in particular communities and applied to the new circumstances of those churches. That which is 'handed on' is proclamation, sacraments and moral life in communion. *The Gift of Authority* interestingly remarks that this is 'at one and the same time the content of Tradition and its result' (18). This could theoretically be 'open-ended' or free rolling. It is not, however, because of the Holy Scriptures.

The Gift of Authority begins its treatment of Holy Scripture unequivocally: 'Within Tradition the Scriptures occupy a unique and normative place and belong to what has been given once for all' (see 19–23). Against the Scriptures the Church has 'constantly to measure its teaching, preaching and action'. The Scriptures are alone the corpus of 'the inspired Word of God'. They are 'uniquely authoritative'. The Old Testament Scriptures were both re-received and re-interpreted as revelation of God's final Word in Christ. The New Testament Scriptures reflect the 'memory' of the people of God being applied in various local situations. The canon of the

Scriptures 'was at the same time an act of obedience and of authority'. This is usefully explained: obedience in the discernment of God's 'Yes'; an act of authority in declaring under the guidance of the Holy Spirit that these and not others were inspired and included. Individual (or private) interpretations of Scripture are subject to the faith of the whole community: 'Word of God and Church of God cannot be put asunder.'

The Gift of Authority examines the question of reception and re-reception (24 and 25), and this is important for the later logic of the document. The re-reception of Tradition, that is the freedom to receive the apostolic Tradition in *new* ways, is an essential part of the picture. Here there is a certain coyness of language. There is a clear recognition of human finitude and sin; a recognition of neglect and abuse. But at what point does abuse become error? The strongest language used is 'inadequate' or 'misleading in a new context'. Though there is a clear and unequivocal recognition of rediscovery and reform (re-reception), the logic and the history would have been strengthened by a plain admission that some things were *wrong*.[4]

The understanding of catholicity in *The Gift of Authority* is helpfully consistent with the Anglican–Lutheran *Niagara Report* (diachronic and synchronic catholicity). Two sentences are of great importance:

> Christ promises that the Holy Spirit will keep *the essential and saving truth* in the memory of the Church, *empowering it for mission* (cf. Jn 14.26; 15.26-27). This truth has to be *transmitted and received anew by the faithful* in all ages and in all places throughout the world in response to the diversity and complexity of human experience (26, emphases mine).

These are crucial sentences in a cardinal paragraph. Had the two highly misleading theological terms 'indefectibility' and 'infallibility' never been coined, the truth they were at best intended to convey is already to be found in those sentences. Yet more accessibly, I believe, to non-Roman Catholic Christians. *Essential and saving* truth will be kept in the memory of the Church (including the Spirit's capacity for re-reception, i.e. reform of abuse and error), and this memory of *essential and saving truth* has indeed been actually applied afresh in each generation and culture (as when Nicaea used a non-scriptural term to defend Gospel truth against Arianism through the use of the term *homoousios* – one substance).

The Gift of Authority explains and expounds its understanding of catholicity further (27–31). Diversity confirms catholicity. The '*people of God as a whole*' is the bearer of this living memory. The Holy Spirit is active in all members of the Church – not least theologians! Bishops, clergy and people *all give and receive from each other*. Each Christian has an intuition of faith (*sensus fidei*). As a whole there is a *corporate sensus fidelium*. The earlier ARCIC material was said to perpetuate a division between clergy/bishops and laity. But *The Gift of Authority* cannot be read in this way, with any careful examination of the actual text, as opposed to a conviction about the past or present Roman Catholic exercise of authority, and should therefore be most welcome to all Anglicans. Though those ordained to a ministry of oversight have a 'ministry of memory . . . as they proclaim the Word, minister the sacraments, and take their part in administering discipline for the common good'(30), this ministry of memory and the wider *sensus fidelium*, of which that ministry is a part, 'exist together in a reciprocal relationship'.

Thus far ARCIC believes Anglicans and Roman Catholics can agree. But we need to retrieve a shared understanding. This will mean trying to understand the best meaning of theological language which is strange or uncongenial. I believe it is a sound, and indeed essential, ecumenical principle always to try to understand theology and practice in another Church in its best possible light rather than its worst. On the same principle, it is good practice to hear a tradition speak for itself rather than place reliance on someone else's caricature articulated for polemical purposes. This is what I mean by a hermeneutic of trust. So when another tradition uses technical language with Latin tags such as *sensus fidei* or *sensus fidelium*, we need to unpack such phrases in a positive way rather than with suspicion. ARCIC helps us in this process with such phrases as 'the ministry of memory'. The *sensus fidei* is therefore helpfully interpreted as 'an active capacity for spiritual discernment, an intuition that is formed by worshipping and living in communion as a faithful member of the Church' (29).

the exercise of authority in the Church

Authority, especially that of those entrusted with oversight, is for mission and unity. Significantly, some of the sharpest debates about authority are raised in missiological contexts. With the expansion of Christianity from a Semitic to a Hellenistic culture huge questions arose in connection with the designation of Jesus the Christ – hence the early councils of the Church and their treatment of Christology and the Holy Trinity, with the consequent development of conciliar authority. So ARCIC naturally leads on to synodality. This is not exactly synodical government as we have it in the Anglican Communion but the *principle* of the whole Church walking along a common way – the way, the truth and the life. Synodality is understood literally as walking together. Anglicans should not make an easy assumption that we have such synodality in perfect form. At the very height of a synodical debate in the General Synod of the Church of England the Registrar calls the Synod to divide, that is to say, to vote. Yet division is the opposite of synodality![5]

From synodality in the local church (diocese) the text moves to the bishop of the local diocese. Some have found the language used here difficult. Phrases like 'binding nature', 'a duty to receive and accept' are not easy for the contemporary Church of England. A contextual interpretation may help. Church people will not have difficulty in gladly recognizing that a bishop can and should exercise authority for the good of the whole community of the Church; for example the churchwarden who asks the bishop to do something about the vicar who is emptying his church; or to persuade a priest to serve from a sense of vocation in an uncongenial parish. Equally, there are the rare but lamentable occasions when the bishop has to exercise discipline after a clerical misdemeanour. There are rare but right occasions when the bishop is required to exercise juridical authority for the sake of the health of the Body of Christ as a whole. Discipline is a mark of the Church of the New Testament and of today.

No diocese is self-sufficient. Synodality (walking together) is required for communion between local diocesan churches. The bishops serve synodality both personally and collegially in many different ways over history and today in all our churches. ARCIC enunciates the principle: 'The maintenance of communion requires that at every level there is a capacity to take decisions appropriate to that level.' Strictly speaking, the only levels Anglicans can 'take decisions' at are the diocesan and the national (provincial). This is our legacy from a nation state Reformation. The sharp theological question this puts to us is: is this an ecclesiological principle; are Anglican Churches for ever tied to the nation state sixteenth-century model? Could there be circumstances in which a wider authority could or should be recognized *for the sake of communion and mission*. At the last Lambeth Conference this was raised in the *Virginia Report*, and, fascinatingly, in the Resolution for an enquiry as to if or when the Archbishop of Canterbury could intervene in another Anglican Church. This was passed by a sizeable majority, some, however, defended as sacrosanct a doctrine of provincial autonomy. Significantly, the historical reason for the Resolution was the desperate situation in Rwanda where there were no authorities left in the Church. Bishops were in prison or in exile, civil war raged and genocide reigned. The Archbishop of Canterbury was morally right to take the action he did in sending in a commissary; as he also did under similar circumstances in the Sudan. The Lambeth Conference commended the Archbishop of Canterbury's intervention! But if morally right why not ecclesiologically right, *under extreme and emergency circumstances*? This is quite different from centralized (ultramontaine) running of dioceses throughout the universal Church from a central bureaucracy in Rome on a day-to-day basis. *The Gift of Authority* could helpfully have brought out this distinction rather more clearly for Anglicans and others. The earlier exercise of primacy by the Roman See was not in relation to day-to-day matters but only in cases of appeal or where, manifestly, a particular church had either erred from the true faith or was subject to disciplinary and organizational chaos. It was only in such circumstances that the early primacy was exercised, other than in the sending of mission to unevangelized peoples, which is a different matter but which also sheds light on *The Gift of Authority*'s understanding of a primacy for mission as well as unity.

Bishops are described in *magisterial* terms; it is worthwhile remembering that Geoffrey Wainwright has said that all Churches have a *magisterium* (i.e. a capacity for and source of teaching authority; for Wainwright this is the Methodist Conference). In the text ARCIC notes the clear teaching role and responsibility of Houses of Bishops in the Anglican Communion with its systems of synodical government. Equally, post *Vatican II* developments are cited within the Roman Catholic Church. Perhaps a more critical approach could have been helpful here, with a little less complacency? Anglican Synods (based on parliamentary models) tend to form a 'government' and 'opposition' mentality. Quite the opposite of 'walking together on a common way'. Equally, the national Roman Catholic Episcopal Conferences have been viewed negatively by the Roman Curia (not having ecclesiological status, according to Cardinal Ratzinger), and the worldwide Synod of Bishops has been both manipulated and sidelined by the Curia. To the suggestion of an ecumenical addition to *ad limina* visits ought to be added the fact of ecumenical consultation and conversation during papal visits; i.e. consultation not only by going to Rome but also when the Pope visits other churches. To some the very term *ad limina* visit would smack of papal autocracy; we need to get behind the word to the idea of one Church visiting another and in the process being in mutual consultation. We are quite familiar with this in other ecumenical contexts such as Churches Together, Councils of Churches and the World Council of Churches. Visits strengthen Churches in mission and witness; for example, delegations from the Church of England to our sister province in Southern Africa during the time of *apartheid*. Once again we need a hermeneutic of trust rather than suspicion in reading this ecumenical text.

Christ has promised that the Christian community will be preserved in essential and saving truth. Indefectibility is therefore properly predicated of the Church only by virtue of Christ's promises (41). I do, however have doubts about the advisability of using the term 'indefectibility' at all. Even to such an intelligent critic as Hugh Montefiore, the earlier ARCIC work on 'indefectibility' was read as 'a Church without defects'. That is to say a Church perfect, without errors or mistakes or abuses. No such Church has ever existed in history, as the NT itself makes patently clear. *Indefectus* means not 'without defect' but rather 'one who has not defected', become a traitor, or apostatized, and therefore ceased to be what they were. Some Christians have maintained that the true Church has died. Such a view requires an episodic ecclesiology. So after sub-apostolic times, for example, the true Church disappeared, only to reappear at the Reformation. But any Church that maintains a view of itself as in *apostolic continuity* with the past must also hold that, by the power of Christ's promise and Spirit, the essential and central saving truths have been maintained in spite of the many serious corruptions and abuses of history. The text might have guarded against such a very widespread misunderstanding of 'indefectibility', which really means the Church as a whole will not die or so proclaim and live untruth as to cease to be the Christian Church.

Moving into yet more disputed waters, we read that the college of bishops with the whole body of the Church, has to exercise a ministry to keep the Church faithful to apostolic Tradition. This is part of their ministry of memory. *The Gift of Authority* more or less recapitulates earlier ARCIC work on councils here. In specific circumstances, assisted by the Holy Spirit, those with this ministry of oversight may come to a judgement, being faithful to Scripture and consistent with apostolic Tradition, which is preserved from error. This is termed 'infallibility' and 'is at the service of the Church's indefectibility' (42). Reams have been and will be written on this. To be responsible, we must take utmost care to listen to what ARCIC is saying *and not saying* here. But ARCIC does not help itself by a lack of exegesis of the term as it understands it or the reality intended behind the term. Crucial are small words or phrases such as 'may', 'faithful to Scripture', and 'consistent with apostolic Tradition'. Critics often cite Article XXI as if it was in contradiction to the work of ARCIC. But

Article XXI also uses the word 'may': 'they *may* err and sometimes have erred.' The logic of the Article is that councils have sometimes erred and have sometimes got it right – as when they have taken things 'out of Holy Scripture', when they may indeed order them as 'necessary to salvation'. Equally, what ARCIC is saying is that sometimes, though not always, councils have been faithful to Scripture and consistent with Tradition; when this has happened we can indeed recognize that they have been assisted by the Holy Spirit. Whether we put the matter positively (as in ARCIC) or negatively (with the Article) the meaning is the same because the word 'may' in both cases implies conditions. ARCIC again uses the word 'may' in explaining the meaning of saying that the 'Church *may* teach *infallibly*'.

ARCIC speaks of such infallible teaching as at the service of the Church's indefectibility. This is very dense indeed and almost to be read as code. In addition to my conviction that such technical Roman Catholic terms are best kept in footnotes if they have to be used at all, some considerable exposition would have helped here. Hans Küng teaches that the Church is 'indefectible' but not 'infallible'. Infallibility, if we are to use the term at all, is only used in strict Roman Catholic ecclesiology of particular decisions or judgements. It is predicated of the Church *as a whole* in *Vatican I* when the Church comes to certain decisive acts of judgement. Put another way, if, on the basis of Christ's promise and Spirit, the Church will never cease to be itself, at least as regards its mission and essential saving truth, there must have been (and can still be) occasions when the Church was assisted by the Spirit and 'got it right' for at least that place and time. At Nicaea (to choose an important but I hope uncontroversial example) the Fathers accepted the *homoousios* and the Christian Church since then has never wanted to reverse that decision. Irreversibility would be a less controversial way of explaining the matter. Few would want to go back on the great conciliar decisions about the person of Christ and the doctrine of the Trinity; though this does not mean they can never be improved or that different cultures do not now require different language.

The *real* problem is not that a council may sometimes be right, but how and when do we know this? Put bluntly, does a definition have authority solely on the basis of its criteria rather than its *criteria and content*? Both are essential and both are unambiguously stated, reception being 'integral to the process':

> Since it is the faithfulness of the whole people of God that is at stake, reception of teaching is integral to the process. Doctrinal

definitions are received as authoritative in virtue of the divine truth they proclaim as well as because of the specific office of the person or persons who proclaim them within the *sensus fidei* of the whole people of God. When the people of God respond by faith and say 'Amen' to authoritative teaching it is because they recognise that this teaching expresses the apostolic faith and operates within the authority and truth of Christ, the Head of the Church (43).

It is here that the dynamic of God's 'Yes' and our 'Amen' is helpful. The 'Amen' is given and welcome when the Church as a whole intuits that Christ is revealed; God's 'Yes' to humanity and the Church. Both 'Yes' and 'Amen' are required: both are ultimately one, interrelated action of the Spirit.

Needless to say, if substantial parts of the people of God decline to give this 'Amen', a question is placed against that particular decision or definition, at least in the form in which it was first expressed. The cautious use of a number of theological terms more familiar to Roman Catholics should not disguise from us the fact that this text puts a radical question mark *against* an automatic, extrinsic or mechanical understanding of conciliar truth.

When all this comes to be applied primatially rather than in a council, ARCIC makes clear that any primatial decision or judgement must still be *collegial*, '*within* the college of those who exercise *episcope* and not outside that college' (47). To help itself ARCIC might have explained what this dense phraseology means. A college of bishops – at whatever level – means communication and exchange of views so that a primate (the Archbishop of Canterbury for example) may on occasion speak for all the bishops, and indeed for the Church as a whole. So at a universal level the primate (who for reasons of history if no more is Bishop of Rome) can only proclaim authoritatively that which is the living faith of the local churches, subject to Scripture and Tradition. The language of paragraph 47 sounds very Roman Catholic. Nevertheless, the content is governed *by all the conditions* already stated for recognizing that a council has proclaimed the faith of the Church: 'This form of authoritative teaching [primatial] has no stronger guarantee from the Spirit than have the solemn definitions of ecumenical councils.'

Was ARCIC disingenuous at this point in relation to more conservative-minded Roman Catholics or Curialists not to restate these conditions? If there is no stronger guarantee from the Spirit (and it is the Spirit here not the authority of the primate) then it is reception, that is the 'Amen' of God's people on recognizing the 'Yes' of God in Christ in the teaching of Scripture in the living Tradition of the Church, which confirms the authoritative decision. Reception does not add authority to a true decision or statement but it shows by the Spirit within the whole people of God that a decision is genuinely authoritative by reason of its content rather than form, by the power of the same Spirit.

All this is followed by a re-emphasis on the fragility of all ministries, including bishops and primates, though stronger language should have been used than 'loyal criticism and reforms are sometimes needed' (48). Similarly, what is said about conscientious dissent could sound too much like an afterthought at this point in the argument. Nevertheless it does link conscience to salvation and human freedom, as well as the responsibility of being a member of the Body of Christ. But it must be emphasized that postmodern individualism should not be equated with a proper Christian respect for conscience and the role of the prophet in the Church.

steps towards visible unity

The Gift of Authority summarizes its agreement and makes a number of practical suggestions by way of steps towards unity. Among them is the fascinating proposal that some form of primacy exercised by the Bishop of Rome could be exercised in advance of full agreement and complete communion. Some critics found this absurd. Yet in many ways this is already happening. The only Christian leader who could with credibility call together a meeting of prayer representing all the faith communities of the world is the Bishop of Rome. And this has happened on two significant important occasions in the present pontificate. Equally the non-Christian world, whether we like it or not, regards the Bishop of Rome as its primary spokesperson and representative. There is a difference between a *de facto* primacy in Christian leadership exercised by the Bishop of Rome and a claim to have the right to organize every local church through the centralized bureaucracy of the Roman Curia. So it is important once again to hear what *The Gift of Authority* is saying and what it is not saying.

There is here, however, a curious omission: there is no direct treatment of the question of jurisdiction. Arguably, jurisdiction is the more fundamental issue, of which an exercise of papal infallibility is a specific and limited instance. It is certainly not said that universal, immediate and ordinary jurisdiction (*Vatican I*) is being recognized while proposing a *provisional recognition* of universal primacy. What is suggested is that Anglicans need some form of wider oversight than a provincial or national Church (56). What is also suggested (57) is that *Vatican II* collegiality has not been sufficiently implemented. This is code for the denigration of episcopal conferences and the world Synod of Bishops mentioned above. There is also a whole list of critical questions for the Roman Curia, which largely exists to give day-to-day implementation to the 'ordinary' jurisdiction of the Bishop of Rome over the other local diocesan churches in communion with Rome. With the Orthodox Churches, Anglicans may wish to find ways of expressing agreement to a form of universal primacy – which might ultimately include some appellate or emergency role on behalf of all the Churches, or which might be exercised through the office of the Archbishop of Canterbury – without the acceptance of the *Vatican I* definition of universal papal jurisdiction. The latter is destructive of any other authority or jurisdiction and changes the bishop of the local Church of Rome into a single bishop over the whole Church. I note that the Lambeth Conference 1988 seemed to presuppose further work on jurisdiction. ARCIC seems to be saying this is not necessary before an advance in relationships, which does not presuppose acceptance of *Vatican I*. The former Archbishop of San Francisco, James Quinn, argues powerfully in his book *The Reform of the Papacy: The costly call to Christian unity* [6] that the practical reform of the Papacy is as essential for unity as theological agreement. The problem with the existing Roman Catholic claims to universal jurisdiction for the Bishop of Rome is that it justifies the day-to-day centralized bureaucracy of which Quinn is so critical as a Roman Catholic Archbishop and ecumenist. Further treatment of the inter-relationship of the Curia to the doctrine of universal jurisdiction would have been helpful.

Nevertheless, silence on jurisdiction means we are not asked to accept this in *Vatican I* terms – which would be impossible for most Anglicans who are inherently Gallican [7] in outlook, the 'heresy' *Vatican I* condemned! What ARCIC seems to be suggesting is that we should consider some recognition of the providential role of the Bishop of Rome as universal primate. Do we have enough agreement on Christ never allowing the gates of Hades to prevail against the Church (which is not the same as saying the Church is perfect) to the extent that the Church fails to be the Church, or that the community of the Gospel entirely fails, to begin to see that for Roman Catholics the primacy has been perceived as an expression of Christ's promises? Can we find an Anglican way of receiving this gift? Can we help Roman Catholics to receive *our* gifts of synodality, emphasizing complimentary reception by the whole Church as an indication of an authentic exercise of authority for mission and truth, as the Early Church received the true councils and rejected false ones?

The imperative of mission in a secularized, postmodern world impels us to whatever degrees or steps or stages of unity a partner can conscientiously agree to. Anomalies can be tolerated if the final vision of visible unity is acceptable, so at least taught the Lambeth Conference in 1998. We shall never be able to move if we want everything on authority settled beforehand. Nor should we expect our ecumenical partners to be just as we want them to be (this is the 'perfect partner syndrome'), i.e. more or less Anglican, before we can advance ecumenically. *The Gift of Authority* offers us a chance of a new way forward, yet only with a hermeneutic of trust rather than suspicion.

chapter five
The Gift of Authority in the Church of England: sketching a contextual theology[1]

Martyn Percy

This chapter explores the question of authority in Anglicanism from a contextual theological viewpoint, with reference to the ARCIC report *The Gift of Authority*. The argument is in three parts, and follows a classical thesis-antithesis-synthesis structure. First, in the thesis, I will sketch the 'practical-prophetic ecclesiology' advocated by Nicholas Healy in his recent work, which claims to be an exercise that focuses 'theological attention on the church's actual rather than theoretical identity'.[2]

Second, in the antithesis, *The Gift of Authority* will be discussed and commented upon in three sections. This will lead to a contextual theological reflection on the nature of Anglicanism and the place of authority within its ecclesiology. Third, in the synthesis, I will make some remarks on the importance of shaping an imaginative contextual theology for the churches which might aid them in their critical self-reflection. Overall, the subtext of this essay suggests that proper attention to cultural studies is an activity that can actually help *redeem* theology, and help save the Church from being emasculated by its own intricate and self-referential rhetoric. Or, as Edward Farley puts it, and to paraphrase, too much modern theology has become ghettoized, and is now a mode of discourse that has slipped into becoming private – a kind of faith monologue that only carries meaning within faith communities, but is losing its place within the public sphere.[3]

In the conclusion I argue that conversations at all levels are part of the methodology of ecumenical ecclesiology. Whilst church leaders and theologians may reach consensus through sophisticated exchanges and finding agreement amongst the subtle nuances of theological vocabulary, such understandings run the risk of establishing a kind of authority that lacks a certain authenticity. In order to dispel this type of problem, grass-roots discussions are suggested and promoted as an integral part of ecumenical methodology.

part one (thesis): Nicholas Healy – against blueprint ecclesiology

Nicholas Healy's prescient work, *Church, World and the Christian Life*, situates the discussion of contemporary ecclesiology between the tension of two poles or traits,[4] namely the tendency on the one hand for theologians to describe the Church in 'ideal terms', whilst on the other failing to address the Church and its problems or possibilities of everyday life – what Healy dubs 'concrete ecclesiology'. Healy argues that the gap between the idealist and the concrete traits tends to inhibit the Church in its discipleship and witness, and, furthermore, stifles the production of a coherent prophetic ecclesiology that might arise out of contextual theologies that pay greater attention to ethnography, sociology and other cognate disciplines. Healy sets about his thesis by exposing the weaknesses of what he terms 'blueprint ecclesiologies'. He writes:

> If we generalize from the wide range of ecclesiological styles of the last century or so, it is possible to detect five key methodological elements. One is the attempt to encapsulate in a single word or phrase the most essential characteristic of the church; another is to construe the church as having a bipartite structure. These two elements are often combined, third, into a systematic and theoretical form of normative ecclesiology. A fourth element is a tendency to reflect upon the church in abstraction from its concrete identity. And one consequence of this is, fifth, a tendency to present idealized accounts of the church.[5]

The discussion proceeds from here, and shows how, for example, an ecclesiologist such as Dulles, in identifying 'models' of the Church such as 'herald' and 'sacrament' (five models in all),[6] allows the models to be used in both explanatory and exploratory ways. Although this approach is initially illuminating, it follows a trend that is common to many modern theologians who reflect on the Church, namely the identification of a 'supermodel' as the pre-eminent way of conceiving of the Church. Thus, for Barth it may be 'the Body of Christ' that is deemed to be denotative; for Rahner it may be 'sacrament'; for Tillard it may be 'communion'.

To this analysis, Healy brings the following insights. First, all 'models' are in some sense deficient – something Dulles acknowledges. Second, the New Testament offers what he calls 'an irreducible plurality of ways of talking about the church'. Third, the doctrine of the Trinity itself requires us to 'keep shifting our perspective[s]', and to acknowledge that no one perspective is ever 'adequate', but, rather, each needs the 'corrective pressure' of another in order to do justice to the rich and multifaceted faith we know as 'Christianity'.[7] As with the Trinity, so it is with the Church; we are bound to a relation of intra-dependent competing convictions in which no one insight or model has supremacy.

This leads Healy to conclude that theologians who deduce a 'complete and normative systematic description of the church from the [a?] definitive model of the church's essence' have missed the point. That is not to say that all 'models' are pointless; it is rather, to say that the models need to be used 'contextually' in ways that aid the exploration of the many facets of the Christian Church. That said, Healy issues further warnings against what he terms 'blueprint ecclesiologies':

> [they] display to some degree a tendency to concentrate their efforts upon setting forth more or less complete descriptions of what the church should ideally become . . . the images and concepts used to model the church are almost always terms of perfection.[8]

The danger of this is that theologians can give the impression that it is 'necessary to get our thinking about the church right first, after which we can go on to put our theory into practice'. As Healy points out, blueprint ecclesiologies therefore *assume* that there can be agreement upon the starting point for a theology of the Church – and of course there is no such agreement, not even in the New Testament. Blueprint ecclesiologies are problematic for other reasons too. In using models of perfection, they fail to distinguish between the Church militant and the Church triumphant, and between the pilgrim Church and the heavenly Church. Blueprint ecclesiologies tend to foster a disjunction between normative theories and accounts of ecclesial practice, and between ideal and concrete ecclesiology, thereby 'undervaluing the theological significance of the genuine struggles of the church's membership to live as disciples within the less-than-perfect church within societies'.

Healy suggests that the deficiencies identified above are best corrected by a proper contextual theology. This is not to separate the Church from its context, but rather, is to recognize that the concrete Church performs its tasks in the world, a place of ever-shifting contexts that inevitably has an impact on shaping its performance.[9] Here Healy pleads for greater attention to the cultural history of the Church, and for ethnography and sociology to help guide the practice of the Church, in order to develop a 'practical-prophetic ecclesiology' that makes use of non-theological disciplines,[10] but without turning away from ecclesiology's primary functions, namely 'to aid the church in its task of truthful witness within a particular ecclesiological context'.[11] Or, as we have been saying, it is important to move away from epic accounts of the Church or blueprint ecclesiologies that 'describe the church in terms of its final perfection rather than its concrete and sinful existence', and from 'normative' accounts or models rather than 'presenting careful and critical descriptions of its activity within the confusions and complexities of a particular theological context'.[12]

To give one practical example, I was recently advising the House of Bishops on some matter, and during the course of our discussion the question of dwindling confirmation rates came up. I pointed out that in Denmark something near 90 per cent of the population continue to be confirmed, whereupon one bishop interjected that we needed to know what Danish theologies of confirmation were about, as we might learn from them. I responded that, whatever differences there might be between Lutheran and Anglican understandings of confirmation, the key to explaining the stark disparity between English and Danish figures would lie in studying culture, sociology, history and ministerial praxis; the key to reversing the decline in England would rest on addressing these factors, not on reconfiguring our theology first, or revising liturgy.

In the next part of this essay I want to *show* how a contextual theological critique can aid an ecclesiology that has settled on the question of authority in the Church *of England*. It does so by paying attention to the cultural history of the Church, and to the grounded or concrete ecclesiology that is part of the lived experience of the Church. In saying this, I am not claiming that the concrete somehow always subverts the blueprint. What I am saying is that The Gift of Authority fails in its ecclesiological task because of its idealist tendencies, and to correct itself it needs to pay more attention to the concrete reality of the Church. Indeed, we could go further here, and point out that a blueprint is, when all is said and done, a theological construction of reality, and not something that is 'revealed'.[13] With these thoughts in mind, we now turn to consider the question of authority in relation to the nature of the Church.

part two (antithesis): *The Gift of Authority* considered

finding authority in a divergent communion[14]

The Gift of Authority is the first ARCIC agreed statement on authority since 1981. A key concept of the report is 'synodality – walking together in the way', which, ARCIC states, finds different expressions in each Church. The Commission stresses the significance of recent trends, and in so doing, presumably condones them. Indeed, the identification of these trends may be seen as the particular nomination of a context (a socio-theological construction of reality might be a better way of putting it), into which the report then 'fits'. These trends are: (1) a reaching towards universal structures that promote *koinonia* (for Anglicans); (2) the strengthening of local and intermediate structures (for Roman Catholics); (3) situating the Church between globalization and localization; (4) the reality of ecclesial subsidiarity. The Commission states that if its new agreed statement is accepted and acted upon, the issue of authority would no longer need to be a cause for continued breach of communion between the two Churches (but see later).

The Gift of Authority also claims to have deepened and extended its agreement on a range of issues, including: how the authority of Christ is present and active in the Church; the role of the whole people of God in the Church, within which the bishops have distinctive voices as teachers in forming and expressing the mind of the Church; synodality, and its implications for the communion of the whole people of God; the possibility, in certain circumstances, of the Church teaching infallibly at the service of the Church's indefectibility; a universal primacy, extended collegially in the context of synodality, as integral to all *episcope*.[15]

Close to the heart of *The Gift of Authority* is the justification for the primacy of the Pope. However, it is important to see that the case for the primacy of the Bishop of Rome is made only on the basis of the document's fundamental ecclesiological presuppositions. As my colleague Ralph Norman notes,[16] the structure of the argument is therefore this: ecclesiology leads to the justification of episcopacy, which in turn, *naturally*, leads to the idea of papal primacy. The infallible primacy of the Pope is, then, only a feature of the broader argument of *The Gift of Authority*; a particular focus for and expression of the ecclesiology that the document assumes.

Norman expands, by pointing out that *The Gift of Authority* defines the Church with reference to 'all those elements that are constitutive of ecclesial communion: baptism, confession of the apostolic faith, celebration of the Eucharist, leadership by an apostolic ministry'. These elements are together referred to as Tradition, that is, 'the Gospel itself, transmitted from generation to generation in and by the Church'.[17] There is one universal Tradition expressed in the Scriptures and administered by the episcopate. It is *complete,* untainted by sin, and remains the same across time and space. Tradition is therefore equated with Truth, that is, God's own Truth, not human truth. 'In the economy . . . of God's love for humanity, the Word who became flesh and dwelt among us is at the centre of what was transmitted from the beginning and what will be transmitted until the end'. Here, it would appear, rests the remainder of the argument. As such, its characteristics should be outlined in greater detail.[18] Critically, it is the substance of Tradition that does not change, but is (re-) received selectively for particular purposes:

> Tradition makes the witness of the apostolic community present in the Church today through its corporate *memory.* Through the proclamation of the Word and the celebration of the sacraments the Holy Spirit opens the hearts of believers and manifests the Risen Lord to them. The Spirit, active in the once for all events of the ministry of Jesus, continues to teach the Church, bringing to remembrance what Christ did and said, making present the fruits of his redemptive work and the foretaste of the kingdom (cf. Jn 2.22; 14.26). The purpose of Tradition is fulfilled when, through the Spirit, the Word is received and lived out in faith and hope. The witness of proclamation, sacraments and life in communion is at one and the same time the content of tradition and its result. Thus memory bears fruit in the faithful life of believers within the communion of their local church.[19]

Norman's reflections on this type of theological language illuminate the principal ecclesial problem: 'the ecclesiology described here is not primarily concerned with the concrete church, in our empirical and temporal world.'[20] The assumption in *The Gift of Authority* is that a doctrinal proposition (the *idea* of Church) is formative and prescriptive of the *concrete* Church. Truth comes from above a *priori*; it does not arise from below a *posteriori*. In other words, the thesis directs the facts. As such, this ecclesiology cannot itself be demonstrated to be true by testing it with the facts of Christian life and liturgy. The method used to settle the question of the Church is by an appeal to authority rather than with persuasive theological argument. In an interesting circularity, the authority of Tradition is therefore established with an appeal to *authority* – and little else. The best we can say here is that method reflects content. At worst, we can

say what we are presented with is a hermetically sealed ecclesiology
or ideology that bears little relation to socio-ecclesial reality.

Anglican ecclesiology

In Stephen Platten's recent *Augustine's Legacy: Authority and
Leadership in the Anglican Communion,*[21] the author offers a
significant and scholarly reflection on the nature of Anglican
identity upon the occasion of the fourteen hundredth anniversary
of Augustine's arrival at Canterbury. How the story of Anglicanism
is told varies according to where the author is standing. Platten
stands within a tradition that is broad, respectful of the past, yet
looking forward. His principal concern is to address the nature of
Anglican authority, and its relationship to individual freedom, place
and the wider Christian context.

As with many studies on Anglican polity, Platten's narration of the
history of the Communion is the vehicle for theological reflection,
and provides the reader with a step-by-step ecclesiology. It is simple,
but effective: Anglicans have been engaging in this type of *apologia*
for centuries. Thus, we have chapters on the local and universal,
the model of commonwealth, authority (naturally), and communion.
Amongst the best work here is the suggestion that Anglicanism is
moving from an appreciation of the Archbishop of Canterbury as
Primus inter pares to a new federalism of *Primates inter pares.*
This is presumably the next phase in ecclesiological subsidiarity
for Anglicans, yet with the Chair of St Augustine remaining a symbolic
focus. In offering this model, Platten sounds a note of caution
against too much centralized power, or any attempt to transform the
office of Archbishop of Canterbury into a pale shadow of the Papacy.
It is no surprise to see interdependence advocated as the successor
to autonomy, with the inductive theological model (with a capacity
for cultural and theological particularity) singled out for praise.[22]

The ethos of *The Gift of Authority* sits uneasily with the kind of
Anglicanism described by Platten, one where it is difficult to identify
confessional documents that describe core beliefs. The Church
of England is a catholic and reformed Church that includes Anglo-
Catholics, conservative evangelicals, liberals – and many who
don't aspire to any of these labels. As a Church, it has traditionally
practised its authority through a trilateral of Scripture, Tradition
and Reason, which has increasingly become a quadrilateral,
encompassing culture (or experience), to take account of the
Communion as a commonwealth that embraces considerable
cultural diversity; authority is often uneasily balanced. There is

diversity within communion, with no strong centralized authority to enforce dogma. The Anglican Communion almost glories in limited doctrinal liberty and liability. Perhaps one could almost say that the Church of England possesses the gift of uncertainty.

As a Church, it is best understood as a *method* – a way of apprehending and comprehending, of looking, rather than the ownership of any essence. Indeed, one could go further here, and say that (following Hooker and others) means are often more important than ends to Anglicans. Anglicanism is a peculiar schooling in *manners* – learning how to agree and disagree with one another, whilst remaining in deep communion. The 'centre' of Anglicanism is seldom found in doctrine, but rather, the manner in which that doctrine is held. As Paul Avis notes:

> interpreters of Anglicanism are sometimes compelled to resort to an appeal to its spirit or 'ethos'. This necessity is often regarded as the Archilles heel of Anglicanism, especially by those – Anglicans or Roman Catholics as the case may be – who require a cut-and-dried propositional statement of Christian truth. But to those who hold to a 'personalist' understanding of truth as a reality that is open to discovery through praxis rather than theory, through Christian life and liturgy, it is certainly not something to be defensive about . . . Fundamental differences there are – but the apparently *insuperable* ones are not of a doctrinal nature. There are differences of 'horizon', of ultimate assumptions regarding the approach to truth and the methods, norms and sources of theology.[23]

In short, Anglicanism recognizes that 'a theological question can only be settled by theological *work*, and not by appeal to authority, in the form of either the *magisterium* or the *consensus fidei*, that would short-cut the process of truth-seeking and enquiry'.[24] At the risk of caricature, what Anglicans might mean by the term 'authority' is naturally different from what Roman Catholics mean by the same. This is because what Anglicans mean by truth is different to what Roman Catholics mean by truth. Although a caricature, it is probable that the essential underlying methodological difference here is an expression of the difference between British Empiricism (with an inbuilt *regard* for scepticism) and Continental Idealism.[25] Empiricism rooted in English spirituality tends to celebrate the limits of human discourse.

Norman makes two points in relation to this. First, there is a danger of building on unresolved theological disputes, and ignoring quite distinctive and different theological cultures: something that *The Gift of Authority* appears consistently to overlook. For example, the claim that Tradition is eschatologically complete, leading, in turn, to the assumption that the episcopate, at all times, possesses the entirety of Tradition, sounds a little odd to Anglican ears. As does a phrase such as: 'The charism and function of *episcope* are specifically connected to the *ministry of memory* . . . Through such ministry the Holy Spirit keeps alive in the Church the memory of what God did and revealed.'[26] Or, that the bishops, acting collegially over time and space, inspired by the Holy Spirit, are infallible, and part of a Church that is spoken of as 'indefectible'. Furthermore, that their judgement is preserved from error because it is an aspect of the eternal, static indefectibility of Tradition (i.e., the *ontological* incorruptibility of something that is eschatologically complete is expressed in the infallibility of the bishops). The point of this language is to establish a foundation: because the bishops guard the Tradition (which is complete), their judgement must necessarily be complete if they are to fulfil the function of *episcope*. But how 'Anglican' is this, exactly? Such political patois, even in the Church of England, is strange and out of character.[27]

Second, Norman shows that further difficulties arise from this. Primacy is presented as a particular expression of the ministry of *episcope*, which in turn reflects and interprets the *sensus fidelium*.[28] In summary, the argument is informed by its methodological presumptions about the *quality* of Truth. Thus, for example, Truth is *assumed* to be single, static and universal: not plural, dynamic and particular. So, *The Gift of Authority* displays what may be described as an idealistic, theoretical ecclesiology 'from above'. Methodologically, it assumes that the task of theology is to seek to understand a conceptual revelation of informative propositions that describe an objective Truth.[29] It assumes that 'appeal to a detailed *magisterium* is the best way of shifting truth from falsity'.[30] This is undoubtedly a coherent Roman Catholic ecclesiology and a clear theological exposition of authority.[31] However, it is not easy to see how this particular 'gift' could be understood or accepted within the wider Church of England, without, for example, *Article xxxvii* of the *Thirty-Nine Articles* rearing its ugly (but important) nationalist head.[32]

culture, context and ecclesial power

I strongly suspect that contextual considerations play a significant part in the rise of idealist traits in Anglican ecclesiology. In the recent volume *To Mend the Net*,[33] bishops Drexel Gomez and Maurice Sinclair tell us that their book is the presentation of a proposal for the exercise of the *enhanced responsibility* that successive Lambeth Conferences have asked the Primates Meeting to fulfil. The Primates are not singled out as the only instrument of unity nor with the idea that they have a monopoly of responsibility or authority. Rather it is because their meeting provides an *authoritative* and *intimate centre, in touch* with the *full circle* of Anglican membership across the world. The proposal challenges some approaches to the practice of provincial autonomy. It contemplates more active decision-making at international level: even hard decisions.[34]

I invite you to note the structure of the argument and its accompanying rhetoric. Who has asked for this kind of authority? Bishops, apparently, asking archbishops – and not a word about the laity. But they are presumably counted as 'the full circle' that the primates are 'in touch with', the primates constituting – with no qualification – an 'authoritative and intimate centre'. In this volume, dispersed authority is inevitably characterized as weak, rendering the episcopal task of oversight and the exercise of authority in matters of faith and order problematic. Correspondingly, Sinclair and Gomez propose an enhanced role for the primates and for the Archbishop of Canterbury, which would give guidance on 'doctrinal, moral and pastoral matters' and, 'while positively affirming the comprehensive nature of Anglicanism . . . exercise a responsibility to specify the limits of Anglican diversity', including the power to intervene in provinces where necessary.[35]

The foundations for the emerging ecclesiology that we have been narrating are complex. A number of recent statements about the Church have tended to Platonize the *koinonia* of the Church (concrete reality), identifying it as a parallel reflection of the *koinonia* of the Holy Trinity (ideal form).[36] Correspondingly, a deep, integrated and ultimately harmonious ecclesial life becomes 'deified', since the life of the Church must reflect the inner life of the Trinity. Yet the effect of this is ironic, for it demonizes all conflict and division as inimical to the life of the Church. Cultural and theological diversity, partiality and incompleteness are cast as ultimate impairments within a Communion, not a source of strength.[37] Inevitably, the agenda of Sinclair and Gomez raises important questions about the Gospel in relation to cultural diversity. The authors are presumably unhappy about some dioceses explicitly rejecting, for example, the Lambeth Conference Resolution on Human Sexuality (1998), and either tolerating or promoting the ordination of practising homosexuals: they believe this impairs communion, or has perhaps already broken the net. Their response is to clarify and intensify episcopal authority, in order to be able to distinguish the 'true' Church from that or those that are in error.

In the context of any serious dispute, finding the right words to reach a political settlement is never an easy task. Words must be found that form the basis of an agreement, even if it is clear to both sides that each party means slightly different things in using the same words. Equally, the architects of such political settlements must be wary that the basis of agreement is acceptable at grass-roots level – that where the politicians can agree, so might the people. The real difficulty with documents such as *The Gift of Authority*, as we have hinted throughout, is that although a form of laudable, top-level ecclesial consensus has been reached, it has been done without wider consent and grass-roots support. This might not matter a jot in the Roman Catholic Church; but it is a more serious issue for Anglicans. Besides which, the Church of England is a special case within the Anglican Communion. It is an established Church, and this places it under particular constraints, as well as affording it opportunities through a binding to certain obligations.[38]

Within the Church of England, it has become fashionable (recently) to emphasize the gift of a threefold order of ministry to the Church: deacons, priests and bishops. This is a Petrine (rather than Pauline) theory of power: authority continues to flow – through lawful succession – originating from the ones whom Jesus has anointed or ordained. This is undoubtedly a gift, to be sure. But to imagine that authority within the Church of England solely resides within these orders is to ignore the complex reality of an established Church. The Queen is the supreme governor of the Church – she is a laywoman. The Prime Minister has a role in key ecclesiastical appointments – he is a layman. Major legislation affecting the Church must pass through the House of Commons: it is *that* 'house of laity', for example, that finally approves measures to ordain women. The people's voice has a decisive role in the people's Church. The bishops may lead, but it is ultimately up to the elected representatives of the people (Members of Parliament in this case) to give their consent.

It remains the case that many laity continue to act as patrons for livings, and can appoint priests to livings against the wishes of a diocesan bishop. Moreover, part of the Church of England's synodality is a General Synod, not a sacred one simply composed of priests and prelates. Even the newly formed Archbishops' Council includes lay representation.[39] Somewhere between Erastianism and Catholicism lies the Church of England: the *via media*. The actual construction of the Church of England reflects another kind of catholicity, one that seeks to be a synthesis between lay and clerical power, faith and doubt, catholic and evangelical, liberal and conservative. Characteristically, this often leads to a Church that is riddled with ambiguity, and is therefore instinctively suspicious of the 'gifts' of authority (whether centralized or symbolic, it is apparently capable of being absolute) and certainty that *The Gift of Authority* seems to offer. The Church of England is still, legally, the people's Church. As a synthesis, it necessarily unites thesis and antithesis. Against this, it is hard to see under what conditions or in what situations the Church of England could deem the authority of the Pope (or a group of primates, no matter how serious the issue) to be greater than that which it already has, and regard that authority as 'indefectible'. The very character of English religion – established in law – suggests that any 'gift' of authority will be perceived and received quite differently in the Home Counties when compared to the cloisters of Rome or the offices of Traditionalist Anglicans in Texas or Sydney.

So, *The Gift of Authority* fails to be effectively ecumenical, because it glosses over the substantial (theological) and real (cultural) differences that remain between Roman Catholicism and Anglicanism. For example, paragraph 61 of *The Gift of Authority* talks about 'a universal primacy of this style' that 'will welcome and protect theological enquiry and other forms of the search for truth'. The use of the word *style* here is curious, for it is personal and transient, not morphologically certain; different Popes have different styles – whose style is meant, exactly? And who says theological enquiry needs protecting – from what, and by whom? Anglican theology could almost be said to *begin* by not being controlled or constrained in the same way that Roman Catholic theology may be: the very idea of an Anglican dogmatics is a contradiction in terms.

The matter of obedience in relation to authority is also problematic. The Papal Encyclical *(Apostolicae Curae)* of Pope Pius XI (1922) describes part of the priestly character as 'an obedience that binds all ranks into the harmony of the Church's hierarchy'. This form of authority is quite alien to an established church where parish priests may enjoy the right of freehold. It remains the case that power is peculiarly dispersed in the Church of England, and that its distribution and control is tied up not in the absolute authority of a bishop, but in legislation and constitution.[40] A further problem with glossy rhetoric in *The Gift of Authority* arises out of its treatment of recognition and reception. The *Apostolicae Curae* of 1896, in which Pope Leo XIII declares 'ordinations performed according to the Anglican rite have been and are completely null and void' remains in force. Despite the encouraging narration of convergence that is present in *The Gift of Authority*, it remains the case that the document asks Anglican bishops to recognize the symbolic primacy of the Pope, whilst the validity of their own ordinations are denied by the same.[41]

At this point, Graham Neville neatly narrates the concrete reality of the Church of England (through social history), rather than some meta-ideological ecclesiology. In so doing, he summarizes the true dilemma for the authors of *The Gift of Authority* in these words:

> The average English Christian (which is to say, the average lay person) seems always to have taken an eclectic approach in matters of belief. Perhaps that is due to the historical experience of the English people in the turmoil of the Reformation period. Today, most church-going members of the Church of England are lukewarm about apostolic succession, but look for reverence in worship. They reject the notion of a collectivist society, but believe that their life in the secular world is the proper place to work out their discipleship. They accept the need for open-mindedness in interpreting and even criticising the scriptures and formularies of religion, but continue to reverence the Bible and to accept the historic creeds, whatever private reservations they may feel about a faith once delivered to the saints and hence immutable.[42]

Whilst English religion continues to remain (at least) something like that which Neville describes, it is hard to see how the authority that is described in *The Gift of Authority* will be understood or accepted by the wider body of the Church of England.

part three (synthesis): sketching a contextual theological critique

Our reflections so far have indicated that insufficient attention to context and culture leads to deficient 'blueprint' theologies or ecclesiologies. But what is to be done to help theologians reflect more broadly and deeply on the life of the Church, doctrine, and on the origins of order and authority? The question goes to the very heart of theological endeavour. Does theology create meanings and narrate worlds and conditions that are yet to come? Or does it reflect on what is given? Or does it try to mediate between these two extremes? As I hinted at the beginning, this is where cultural studies (which include ethnography and the social sciences) might begin to help theology. But is the recipe I am hinting at here a proper 'contextual' theology? I think so, in so far as we are trying to pay proper attention to experience, refusing to divide culture from tradition, critiquing idealism, and beginning to edge towards a critical reflection on praxis. In this respect, the approach of Healy, although centred on ecclesiology, is clearly a form of contextual theology, in which truth, revelation and transformation emerge in praxis and synthesis more faithfully than they might in hermetically sealed idealism. Thus, although theologians are often divided on the use of social sciences in terms of providing an account of the Churches and the practice of Christian life, Healy claims:

> All forms of social science are useful, perhaps even necessary for ecclesiology, including those that are thoroughly antagonistic to the church or to religious bodies generally. However, since they examine religious bodies in a variety of ways, they cannot be useful in quite the same way, and none of them is ever normative.[43]

That some social scientists are now prepared to acknowledge their disciplines as interpretative rather than complete descriptors and analyses of religion affords an opportunity for theology and the social sciences to collaborate in their readings of Church and society.[44] This may lead to what Healy describes as 'practical-prophetic' ecclesiology, which might arise out of a particular way of reflecting on the Church in the world:

> Ecclesiological forms of history, sociology and ethnography, in debate with parallel non-theological disciplines, may help the church live more truthfully by drawing critical attention back to the confusions and complexities of life within the pilgrim church. Practical-prophetic ecclesiology acknowledges that Christian existence is never stable or resolvable in terms of purely theoretical constructions, but is ever-moving, always struggling along with the theodrama. It acknowledges too that the church must engage with other traditions of enquiry not only for their sake, but for its own, in order that it may on occasion hear the Spirit of the Lord in their midst.[45]

Whilst such confidence is not without its caveats, a primary task for contextual theology (or Healy's practical-prophetic ecclesiology) might be this: to argue for an interrogative and empathetic theological engagement with contemporary culture, for the sake of culture, and for the sake of the Church. The point of a contextual theological engagement with the contemporary is therefore partly an appreciative and missiological exercise. The Churches need to continually receive the Holy Spirit, already present and accommodated in culture and beyond the Church, and what the Spirit is saying outside the Church to the body of Christ beyond its immediate distinct and bounded existence (assuming one can ever even agree on where the Church begins and ends). On the other hand, there is also a task to make theology as public as possible, in order that the voice of the Spirit may be heard. As David Tracy notes:

> Theology, by the very nature of the kind of fundamental existential questions it asks and because of the nature of the reality of God upon which theology reflects, must develop public, not private, criteria and discourse . . . all privatisation, all refusals to face action, praxis, politics, history are fatal not only to theology but to the proclamation and the manifestation of the event of Jesus Christ that empowers theology.[46]

For Tracy, theology is not to be considered as a mode of reflection that is culturally marginal: it is, rather, a part of culture. Correspondingly, the particularity of theology should not be confused with the realm of the 'private': every public discourse is particular, and 'all theology is public discourse'.[47] This involves openness at the very heart of the theological endeavour.[48] Taking cultural development seriously is therefore beginning to emerge as a major theological and ecclesiological task. Paul Lakeland exemplifies this when he writes:

> the moment of theological outreach to the wider human community . . . needs *mediation* if its message is to be heard. But at the same time it brings secular wisdom to the aid of the faithful community itself . . . thus, the theologian taken up with this fundamental moment will be deeply immersed in the cultural and intellectual processes of the age. Cynics might consider this today to be a thankless task, but it is arguably the only way in which mediation can occur.[49]

Lakeland's work is intriguing on a number of counts, for it rejects both the post-liberalism of scholars such as Lindbeck, as well as the countermodernity of Milbank. Lakeland argues for a deeply dialogical engagement with the world that is characterized by humility, salience, openness and rigour. Kathryn Tanner expresses the agenda like this:

> The basic operations that theologians perform have a twofold character. First, theologians show an artisanlike inventiveness in the way they work on a variety of materials that do not dictate of themselves what theologians should do with them. Second, theologians exhibit a tactical cleverness with respect to other interpretations and organisations of such materials that are already on the ground . . . The materials theologians work on are incredibly diverse . . . theologians use a kind of tact requiring numerous ad hoc and situation-specific adjustments. In contrast to what the values of clarity, consistency and systematicity might suggest of themselves, even academic theologians do not simply

follow logical deductions where they lead or the dictates of abstract principles when arriving at their conclusions. They do not construct their theological positions by applying generalities to particular cases, or emend them by trying to reproduce the same clear meanings in the terms of a new day, so as to convey them across putatively accidental differences in circumstances and vocabulary. Instead, they operate by tying things together – the Latin meaning of *religare*, after all, is to bind.[50]

Tanner's description of theological method is one of skilled and discerning appropriation. Indeed, the description resonates with the ways in which cultural studies and theology can describe themselves: 'a collective term for diverse and often contentious intellectual endeavours that address numerous questions'.[51] Theology is, in reality, a collection of disciplines, which ranges over vast fields, and Tanner works with a concept of religion ('tying things together'), which reveals her own view about the relations between culture, tradition and revelation. Tanner's world is one where theology is both part of culture as well as a discipline that can step outside it; foundationalist and non-foundationalist.

Discerning engagement is clearly a key – an *interrogative theology* that is formed by wisdom, which listens as well as speaks. Theology cannot only be concerned with the maintenance of the Church. Theology has its own imperative to reach beyond itself in the pursuit of wisdom, and seeks wider social flourishing and cultural nourishment. I have already alluded to the similarities between theology and cultural studies, and suggested that understanding theology as a 'collection of disciplines', or perhaps more accurately as a *collation*, can free the discipline to be more engaging and adventurous. Contextual theology can be critically reflective, practical-prophetic, culturally alert, transformative, evocative and celebratory. The approach can, in short, reflect the abundance, generosity and inclusivity of their subject; which is only to allude again to religion, and the reality and mystery of God.

The approach outlined here can also, perhaps, go one stage further. The title of this chapter uses the word 'sketching', and intentionally pulls away from the more precise notion of drafting a blueprint. If only analogically, and following Tanner's oblique reference to the theologian as artist, I am suggesting that contextual theology can be a form of illuminating portraiture that attempts to capture and transform reality in ways that may be liberating and suggestive; it does not proscribe as blueprints do. In blueprints, the primary colours are laid out, and although they may intersect, they retain their distinctive hue. In portraits, colours are blended together, creating new shades and perspectives. Contextual theologies do not provide patterns to follow; they are pictures to inspire.[52]

conclusion

I am conscious that in reading back this essay, some may detect more than a faint whiff of English parochialism – a fear of collaboration with 'foreign' partners, and a resistance to 'alien' ideals. Suffice to say, it has not been my intention to stoke up the fires of Anglicanism 'against the tyranny of Rome': nothing could be further from my heart or mind. In setting about the essay in this way, I have not meant to lack in generosity; there are many fine sentiments in *The Gift of Authority*, and I would be amongst the first to say that the work deserves to be widely read and appreciated. So why is my essay set out in the way that it is? Three brief points need making by way of conclusion.

First, there must be a link between *authority* and *authenticity*. The two words are, of course, closely related. But on balance, the authentic is linked to the genuine, real, actual and that which is of established credit. It is the authentic that, by its nature, is entitled to respect. Authority also involves the capacity to command respect and obedience; it gains its supremacy by right.[53] But what happens when authority and authenticity become divorced? The real becomes separated from the (enforced) ideal; policy is out of step with praxis; the genuine no longer corresponds to the imagined. What mostly concerns me about *The Gift of Authority* is that it pays so little attention to the *actual* nature of Anglicanism (which I know is contested). It is for this reason that Healy's work prefaces the whole discussion; a focus on the concrete Church actually helps the *blueprint* ecclesiologies to enable a more faithful witness. It is for precisely this reason that important cultural differences between the Church of England and Roman Catholicism are not ignored. More often than not, such 'cultural distinctives' are not peripheral, ephemeral artefacts, that matter little; rather, the objects, beliefs and practices are valued and cherished, and are part of the material economy of salvation that is deeply embedded in the socio-theological life of a given ecclesial community.

Second, the style of the cultural and theological sketch should alert the reader to the fact that gifts are part of the economy of exchange. What does the giver receive in exchange for giving the gift? I have been unable to detect what, if anything, the Roman Catholic Church might receive from Anglicans were they (i.e., Anglicans) minded to accept *The Gift of Authority*. I do not see a necessary reciprocal relationship articulated in the ARCIC Report; Anglican orders, for example, continue to remain 'null and void'. In the economy of exchange, it is reasonable to expect gifts to be given and received in a spirit of mutuality. Whilst it may be true (and contrary to my earlier narration) that Anglicans may need to learn to receive something of the otherness from an 'alien' tradition, welcoming the diversity and richness that the import brings, the equation surely has to balance. In short, what riches from Anglicanism or the Church of England will be welcomed and embraced by Roman Catholics? Does an agreement on authority (of all things) really *deepen* our life together?

Third, the appeal for a grounded contextual theological approach is a call for the work of ARCIC to continue – but at grass-roots level. All too often, ecumenical dialogue can appear to be a specialist discourse that only the most able and diplomatic theologians can undertake. And yet the experience of many ecumenical partnerships at the local level may have much to say to those who continue dialogue at 'higher' levels. On the ground, so to speak, questions of authority are often less intense and more contingent. Is not the Holy Spirit active in these conversations and relations? Can the Churches not learn from their own grassroots? The answer is presumably 'yes'. In which case, future ecumenical dialogues on the nature and gift of authority should take account of context, history, culture, the voice of the laity, and the delightful ambiguities of the concrete Church, but *not forgetting* the certainties of ecclesiological blueprints. They need each other. A wider, more authentic and real conversation is the only way in which *The Gift of Authority* could be truly understood and received. This would, of course, mean more theological work at local, regional and national levels, and more frankness about difference, perceptions of reality, ideology, and attention to style and substance.

If the 'engagement' that is being mooted in *The Gift of Authority* is to get even halfway down the aisle, it is perhaps best to have these 'real' conversations before we get to the altar. There is a wise old English proverb: 'Marry in haste, repent at leisure.' Obviously no one is suggesting that *The Gift of Authority* is not a careful piece of theological work: it is. However, *The Gift of Authority* clearly proposes a kind of marriage; but before any engagement can be announced, we need some more talking – at all levels. Such conversations are vital to the heart, mind and purposes of authentic ecumenical theology and its methodologies.

chapter six

it's the thought that counts: reflections from local contexts in England

Flora Winfield

opening the box

> The trouble with beautifully wrapped presents is that when you open the box you sometimes find something rather unexpected inside. The gift you're given isn't always the gift you expect; even your friends sometimes surprise you with something you don't like or want or which isn't to your taste.

This response, from a lay person in a Local Ecumenical Partnership, sums up something of the reaction from many local contexts to *The Gift of Authority*. In searching out responses to *The Gift*, I found less than positive reactions from many people who had received the earlier ARCIC texts with interest and even with enthusiasm.

A number of questions emerged from my search for responses among Anglicans and Roman Catholics engaged in the ecumenical process:

- What does it mean for our life together, in which our unity in Christ is beginning to be made visible, that we agree on these things?
- How is this agreement related to our shared life and experience?
- How will this agreement call and enable us for new ways of living the life of the Church? How will it change us?

Anglicans and Roman Catholics work together in a great variety of contexts in England: in some places the relationships are long-established, mature and have become an accepted aspect of how each Church carries out its daily life and ministry. In others relations are at best distant and polite, at worst suspicious. It is difficult to make generalized comments about the nature of the Anglican–Roman Catholic relationship in parishes and local communities, except to say that everywhere bears the distinctive marks of history, geography and local personality and that these are often the factors which shape inter-Church relationships, rather than questions of ecclesiology or authority. However, in almost every situation, Anglicans and Roman Catholics relate to one another not in bilateral isolation but in the context of a complex web of relationships with a whole range of other ecumenical partners – in particular the Methodists but also United Reformed, Baptists, Quakers, Salvation Army, Black Majority Churches and Orthodox.

saying yes and hearing no

> God's gift of authority to his Church is at the service of
> God's 'Yes' to his people and their 'Amen'. (Preface to *The
> Gift of Authority*)

In my search for responses, there were those who said that they, as inter-Church families, ecumenically involved lay people or clergy, did not feel that the stuff of the report was the stuff of their lives. They asked: 'Does this text describe the Churches as we know them?' In earlier reports, which they had studied together in the light of their own contexts, they had been able to identify the tangible connections between the dialogue's work, on for example sacraments or ministry or life in Christ, and their own daily experience of the Church's brokenness. But *The Gift* suffers on a number of counts: authority exercised within the Church is often perceived as a negative, constricting force, imposed rather than received. In an increasingly non-deferential culture, authority is not, for many people, a positive term; it is not a 'Yes' word. Where the authority of the Churches touches lived, inter-Church experience, where it touches life, it is often heard to say 'No'.

For some, the description of the Church in the text sounds just too distant, too idealized and too much like a community of agreement to be of real help to them in their daily ecumenical living. As they constantly encounter the broken and divided Church, they long not only for the healing of division, but also for the reflection in the authoritative structures of the Church of a proper theological approach to disagreement, and to the task of coming to a common mind in a way that embraces an understanding of the legitimate place of diversity in the Church.

For others, the central difficulty with the text was that they simply did not believe that either their own or the partner Church was open to being changed, in relationship, on these questions. Stereotypes are sometimes a factor here, and we need to work consciously to overcome them: the caricatures include not only how those in each

Church view those in the other, but also how people from both Churches see both hierarchies. Viewed 'from beneath', the sight of authority being exercised is not always edifying. In spite of the frequently restated public commitment of both Churches to discovering and making visible the unity that is God's gift, it remains the case, in some ways puzzlingly so, that many of those who live out the Churches' ecumenical vocation in their daily life feel that they are not truly owned by their own Churches. There are questions here not only about making unity visible but also about making the exercise of authority more visibly a gospel activity.

experiences of living in dialogue

local belonging

In many local contexts, Anglicans and Roman Catholics have been living their dialogue for years and there is a developing sense of belonging together, often located in a particular context for ministry, a place, an area of common mission, a shared spirituality. When the Church of England collected responses to the Churches Together in England process, Called to be One, in 1997, one of the strongest themes to emerge was this experience of belonging together across ecclesial boundaries; people expressed their experience of having things in common which were more significant than their denominational allegiances. In particular this was expressed as common mission to a place. This sense of community, of located common belonging as Christians, depends on and is held together by a sense of common purpose and calling to witness and service. This is often expressed as an experience of common life.

mutuality and participation

As ecumenical relations in local contexts have grown and matured over the years, distinctive patterns of church life in England have developed, which are characterized by gifts given and received, by an expectation of mutuality and of active participation. These patterns of church life are not, of course, taking place apart from the process of theological conversation which has accompanied their development over the past fifty years. The work of ARCIC and of other international and national bilaterals, and in particular the convergences of the BEM process, has informed, encouraged and enabled this developing shared life, where people in local contexts bear witness to and live out something of the unity discovered in the work of the dialogues.

Authority is about how the Church teaches, acts and reaches doctrinal decisions in faithfulness to the Gospel, so real agreement about authority cannot be theoretical. If this statement is to contribute to the reconciliation of the Anglican Communion and the Catholic Church and is accepted, it will require a response in life and deed. (Preface to *The Gift of Authority*)

Questions of authority, of ecclesiology, *episcope* and episcopacy, discipline and synodality do arise in local ecumenical work, but are not often perceived or articulated as questions of authority. Years living and working alongside one another in close and committed ecumenical relationships in England have shaped our ideas and expectations. People have grown accustomed to the idea that being in relationship is about listening to and growing towards other traditions, and structures have developed which enable the churches to take counsel together, structures which assume the participation of clergy and lay people together.[1] Both Anglicans and Roman Catholics have, through these developing relationships, encountered different patterns for expressing authority among their partner churches.

giving and receiving gifts

Conversation is always about the volume of listening as well as the volume of speaking. To be in dialogue is primarily to attend to God's work in the life, history and experience of a tradition different from your own, to encounter difference with the intention of hearing the other tradition, and with the awareness that to be in dialogue is to be open to the Holy Spirit, who is at work in your relationship, in the space between divided Churches. Being in conversation is also about being open to being changed together, transformed by the Spirit's work towards the Church into which God is calling us.

When Christian communities are in real but imperfect communion they are called to recognise in each other elements of the apostolic Tradition which they may have rejected, forgotten or not yet fully understood. Consequently, they have to receive or reappropriate these elements, and reconsider the ways in which they have separately interpreted the Scriptures. Their life in Christ is enriched when they give to, and receive from, each other. (31)

This process of giving and receiving is also not only about recognizing the Church in another tradition, but also about knowing your own tradition in new ways, as you share it and come to see it afresh through others' eyes. This means bringing to the table not only those things that delight and inspire us, but also looking with a new perspective at those aspects of our inheritance that cause others to be troubled or afraid. In both the conversation that takes place around the dialogue table and the conversation of our shared life, we are called to receive one another's traditions as gifts. If we take our dialogue partners seriously, this means that we must also look carefully at the gifts we seek to offer others.

healing memories

People working in local contexts and living across the churches' divisions encounter daily the painful reality that they are serving the bread of life from broken tables. The brokenness of the churches often still reflects the divided nature of the human community. The churches are divided not only by theological disagreement, but also by race, class, history, memory, culture and geography. The account of authority offered in *The Gift* touches on these concerns: 'When the churches, through their exercise of authority, display the healing and reconciling power of the Gospel, then the wider world is offered a vision of what God intends for all creation' (50).

The unity of the Church is important not only for the sake of the Church but also for the sake of a broken world.

How can the theological dialogues discover ways of attending more closely to the experience of living towards being the 'all in each place', so that the theological insights of these places can, in turn, inform, encourage and enable the 'all in every place'? Even if the churches found themselves to be in complete agreement on the nature of *The Gift of Authority*, they would still find themselves divided, by race, class, history, memory, culture and geography. Living in dialogue in local contexts, across these divisions, has begun this work of reconciliation and as well as reading the text, we need to learn together to read these contexts: what can we glimpse of the Spirit at work in their life together?

When churches are in dialogue, they engage in a process of mutual conversion. Not in seeking to change their partner to become more like themselves, but in bearing witness to one another to the Holy Spirit's transforming work in their relationship. To be in dialogue is to be vulnerable to one another, and to the Spirit's work; as we offer one another the treasured gifts of our traditions we risk rejection and misunderstanding. *Kenosis* is at the heart of the process of dialogue, and characterizes true encounter with difference. Working with ecumenical partners is often a painful and difficult business, and requires the development of structures for the exercise of authority which are able to provide a framework within which the life of the Church, in all its diversity, can flourish. In dialogue, churches also come to recognize that each lacks what the other has, and that they need one another.

receiving the gift

Agreement on matters of authority is vital, undergirding all other aspects of the ecumenical process, but such agreement must also reflect the reality of the churches' lives and relationships if it is to be credible and to be received.

The texts produced by the work of ARCIC over the years have, as with any long-standing dialogue, reflected the changing membership of the group and the developing relationships of the people involved as well as of the churches who sent them. The texts of a dialogue are the fruit of life in community and in communities: the community which grows among those in conversation, and the communities which flourish among those from different Christian traditions who live and work together in local contexts. It is in the lives and experience of these wider communities that the conversation needs to take root: for Anglicans and Roman Catholics to be in conversation, there needs to be a conversation everywhere that there is an Anglican and a Roman Catholic.

chapter seven
in conclusion . . .

Peter Fisher

There are many ways of unpacking: look around the living room after present-opening time at Christmas to know that. This collection has offered different views of *The Gift of Authority* and, indeed, different ways of 'getting at' the meaning and value of the text. But, having done the unpacking – in various ways – what, now, do we make of the gift? This concluding chapter is in three parts. The first presents a survey and analysis of what has gone before; the second suggests some other perspectives on the text and its subject; the third considers the question, where do we go from here?

a backward glance

This collection is, at one level, an exercise in hermeneutics (or interpretation). Christians are well used to this. The faith and life of a disciple grows and develops as a kind of 'interpretation' of Scripture, as we ask ourselves, 'What did Jesus (or Paul, etc) mean by this?', and, 'What does it mean in this situation?' The New Testament itself encourages the reader to take texts seriously – always assuming that making good sense of the text will lead to good actions.[1]

But what is it to take this text – *The Gift of Authority* – seriously? Some[2] have argued for a sympathetic reading, adopting a 'hermeneutic of trust', and putting the best construction we can on the sincere statements of brothers and sisters in Christ. This, after all, is how we try to listen to our friends. It is also a natural approach to adopt in seeking reconciliation or the resolution of conflict. We know that many people (perhaps British people, particularly) tend to be suspicious and dismissive about ideas and forms of speech that are unfamiliar. This tendency feeds and fosters entrenched divisions between Christians – especially between 'Catholics' and 'Protestants'.[3] And how can suspicion ever be dissipated unless the suspicious parties determine to listen with reconciling ears?

In his historical introduction, Stephen Platten reminds us of the history of reconciling listening that lies behind *The Gift*, and that has characterized the long patient process of Anglican–Roman Catholic dialogue. With the same history in mind, Christopher Hill's essay invites us to remember the high aspirations and generous language of the document, to remember the need to make compromises to win the goal of Christian unity and to consider the folly of those who live in glasshouses (perhaps – in this case – rather vulnerable, Anglican glasshouses) throwing stones. Mary Tanner's essay, too, offers a sympathetic reading of *The Gift*, but (like Christopher Hill's) it shows that a hermeneutic of trust need not rule out criticism. The implicit plea of these essays is that all who care for Christian unity should respond warmly to this latest fruit of international dialogue and should do all in their power to ensure that its forward momentum is maintained, when it could so easily be lost.

Others[4] have taken the text seriously by arguing or disagreeing seriously with it – something we may also do with friends! They, we might say, have adopted a 'hermeneutic of suspicion' in approaching the text. However, the contrast should not be made too baldly. Even the most questioning and critical writers in this collection have striven to be fair (not just suspicious) toward the document and its aspirations, and to place their contributions in the context of the wider goal of unity. But still, in their more critical tone, the essays by Martin Davie and Martyn Percy raise important questions about how we carry forward ecumenical dialogue (or any other conversation aimed at reconciliation). After all, trust can be said to rest on candour, and to grow by the mutual probing of conversationalists who dare to voice disagreement and doubt. And what if the consensus that appears in an ecumenical document like *The Gift* is in some way incomplete? It might be incomplete in leaving some properly interested groups 'out in the cold', or in ducking some significant issues, or – perhaps most damagingly of all – in failing to represent truthfully the faith and life of the participant Churches. If such were the case, surely plain speaking is the only remedy?

In this collection, *The Gift* has been criticized for failing to do justice to key features of Anglican understanding, for its idealization of the (messy) reality of the Church, and for the style and character of its theology. In every case, those who have offered these criticisms have also noted what they regard as good features of the document; they have also expressed their commitment to the advancement of unity between the Anglican and Roman Catholic communities of faith.

The contributors to this volume have done us two important favours. They have taken the trouble to look closely at the text of *The Gift of Authority*, and they have stated their own views and interpretations in such a way that thoughtful readers will be able to evaluate and weigh them. The aim of the exercise is that the widest range of people who care about unity and about the proper exercise of authority in the Church should continue this process in the same way: attending to the vitally important text and carrying forward the debate that arises from it with the same care, clarity and openness.

Yet this may be a lot to ask, perhaps too much. It seems, judging by Flora Winfield's survey of local ecumenical opinion, that church members have found it difficult to respond to *The Gift*. Two of the reasons for this merit special attention here.

First: authority is the *last* subject we want to talk about today. Or, more accurately, it is the last subject to which we wish to give positive consideration. In everyday thinking, we tend to make no distinction between 'authority' and 'power', and we habitually follow the news media in associating both with automatic corruption (following Acton's famous dictum, 'Power tends to corrupt'). Words that are traditionally linked with authority in the Church – like 'hierarchy' and 'magisterium' – are more likely to arouse sceptical or cynical instincts than pious ones. ARCIC, on the other hand, has consciously swum against this tide in its work on authority: as the Anglican Co-chairman, Bishop Mark Santer said on presenting the report: 'We do not collude with the common idea that all authority is corrupt.[5] So, in place of the customary debunking of authority (customary, at least in Britain), the report takes authority to be 'a gift' and a relatively uncomplicated blessing for the Church. There is a gulf, then, between the ways issues of authority are dealt with on the street – or even in the pew – and how they are dealt with in the report.

Yet it must surely be worth making the effort to bridge this gulf. A serious and balanced debate on authority in the Church is, potentially, of value not only to the Church itself but also to the wider society. In her Reith Lectures for 2002, Onora O'Neill presented a fascinating diagnosis of the apparent 'crisis of trust' and the accompanying 'culture of suspicion', which characterize contemporary public life in Britain. She observes how journalists now treat it as almost self-evident that: 'Mistrust and suspicion have spread across all areas of life . . . Citizens, it is said, no longer trust governments, or politicians, or ministers, or the police, or the courts, or the prison service.'[6] Interestingly, her analysis is that the 'crisis of trust' is more imagined than real: we are living in a strangely schizophrenic society in which people still repose actual trust in those who hold authority, whilst publicly subscribing to the view that authority cannot be trusted. My own observation (not Dr O'Neill's) is that the situation she describes so acutely is one in which a mature discussion about how authority should be granted, held and exercised *cannot* take place. The churches, for their part, whilst not isolated from the wiser culture of mistrust, yet retain a profound belief that true authority can be given and recognized, even on earth. Consequently, they can and should engage keenly in their own ecumenical debate about authority, with at least half an eye on the implications of this debate for society as a whole.

The second point is linked with the first. Partly because it is not easy for us to think and talk about the due place and nature of authority, we tend to disguise or camouflage its reality when it obtrudes at family or local community level. There are, no doubt, still parents or priests who 'lay down the law', but perhaps more frequent are those who actually hold some domestic or congregational authority but constantly play it down or deflect questions concerning it to someone 'higher up' and out of sight. This habit contributes to the sense that issues about authority are not a problem for 'us' in 'our locality', but are thrust upon us from outside or from above. *The Gift of Authority* almost colludes with this preference for evacuating the local sphere of any recognizable exercise of authority by concentrating so decisively on the role of bishops. Yet the positive teaching of *The Gift* about the interdependence of the whole people of God and those called to a ministry of *episcope* in the exercise of authority could usefully be applied to the local and congregational realm – and explored and critiqued as a model for the good conduct of the local and neighbourhood church.

listening for other voices

This collection of essays is, inevitably, *selective*. What precisely was the basis for the selection of contributions? Contributors were chosen to represent a wide range of views from among those in the Church of England known to be closely concerned with ecumenical theology generally and with the issues raised by *The Gift of Authority* in particular. Each had already published some written comment on the report, and, in some cases, the essay printed here has drawn on this earlier work. Meanwhile, Flora Winfield, as Local Unity Officer of the Council for Christian Unity, was asked to gather reactions to the report from those involved in ecumenical relationships 'on the ground'.

Another collection could have embraced many other perspectives. Most obviously, it could have included contribtions from other Churches. Had this been practicable it would surely have been beneficial. However, this collection reflects the main purpose of the publication – to encourage a mature and wide-ranging reflection on *The Gift of Authority* among Christians, especially in the Church of England. It also gives an indication of the range of voices *usually* heard in informed discussion of ecumenical issues in the Church of England. Varied as the voices are, the discussion remains – in important ways – a limited one. Yet the very word 'ecumenical' implies the widest possible conversation.[7] So it seems important that we should make the conscious effort to listen for some of the 'voices off' that might broaden this conversation, even though we cannot expect to 'speak for them' adequately.

Feminist and Liberation Theology perspectives are among those seldom heard in ecumenical discussion: so it is with this collection. In themselves, these represent wide realms of theological exploration and debate, so it would be foolish to generalize about 'a feminist view' or a 'liberationist view' of *The Gift*. However, there are a number of pressing questions that are consistently raised by theologians in these groups, and it may be that some of these questions are either absent from or under-represented in the conversation of this book. Most obvious would be a range of questions about power, its use and abuse, and its relation to authority.

Many feminist writers, among others, have argued that the Churches retain patriarchal patterns of social order and that these patterns do not fit with the distinctive message and dynamic of the Gospel. These authors see traditional Church order as patriarchal. Rosemary Radford Ruether defines patriarchy as, 'a historically contrived social system by which "the fathers" – that is, middle-class males – have used power to establish themselves in a position of dominance over women and also over dependent classes in the family and society'.[8]

Developing the concept of patriarchy in relation to the Churches, Letty M. Russell contrasts a patriarchal understanding of 'authority as domination' with 'authority as partnership'.

> In this understanding of authority as domination, things are assigned a divine order, with God at the top, men next, and so on, down to dogs, plants and 'impersonal' nature. Theological 'truth' is sought through ordering the hierarchy of doctrines, orders and degrees. The difficulty for women and third world groups is that their perspectives often do not fit in the pyramid

structures of such a system of interpretation. . . . Anyone who persists in raising questions and perspectives that do not fit the paradigm pays the price of further marginalisation.[9]

In contrast, Russell (with other feminist theologians) posits an understanding of authority as partnership, which involves a shift from 'Jacob's ladder leadership to leadership in the form of Sarah's circle':[10]

> In this view, reality is interpreted in the form of a circle of interdependence. Ordering is explored through inclusion of diversity in a rainbow spectrum that does not require that persons submit to 'the top', but rather that they participate in the common task of creating an interdependent community of humanity and nature. Authority is exercised *in* community and not *over* community.[11]

These observations are addressed to the Churches generally, and not to the specific model of authority set out in *The Gift*, so care needs to be taken to consider not only the intrinsic force of the critique, but also whether it applies justly to part or the whole of this model. Inevitably and naturally, the challenge they offer relates not only to the structural hierarchy of the Churches (Anglican and Roman Catholic, in this case), but also to the exclusion of women – and, it may be, the under-representation of other groups in society – from existing roles of leadership in the Church.

A different kind of lack, a missing element in this conversation, arises through the absence of a specialist biblical scholar amongst the contributors. Here again, this collection represents the wider community of those who write about ecumenism: most are not biblical scholars. Yet *The Gift*, like all such documents, both employs Scripture and discusses the role of Scripture. In fact the theology of *The Gift* takes its starting point from two verses in Paul's second letter to the Corinthians (2 Corinthians 1.19-20). So it is particularly interesting to see a biblical scholar's perspective on the document.

Such a perspective is offered by Dr Joy Tetley, in a paper about the use of the Bible in ecumenical dialogue. She comments about the report's use of this text:

> Having stressed that the Scriptures emerged from and are related to specific contexts, *The Gift of Authority* (in common with other dialogues) does not work out the implications of this when making use of Scriptural references in the text as a whole. This is certainly true of its key biblical text, 2 Corinthians 1. 19-20. It is extracted from its Pauline context (Paul defending himself and his

proclamation of the Gospel) and applied to the various matters to do with authority raised in the Statement. There is, to say the least, a debate to be had as to whether Paul's words can be stretched that far.[12]

In the same paper, after analysing a number of ecumenical texts, she comments on the general quality of their treatment of the authority of Scripture.

> All the dialogues regard the Bible as normative and fundamentally authoritative. What is lacking, however, is a sustained exploration of what this might mean, and how the range of terminology used might be understood. A word like 'inspired', for instance, can have a variety of senses, depending on context and assumptions.[13]

'There is a debate to be had.' Those who have laboured for years to forge an ecumenical consensus and to find words to express it in *The Gift* might well hear those words with some weariness or disappointment. For time and again the carefully crafted planks of ecumenical agreement have turned out to be springboards for new debate *as well as* steps on the long staircase to visible unity. All that has been offered in these last paragraphs is a hint as to two of the areas in which further debate ought to take place.

where do we go from here?

This collection will have succeeded if it conveys the sense that *The Gift of Authority* is not an inert, lifeless text – a testimony to other people's preoccupations – but is alive with questions and concerns that cry out for our continuing attention.

There are many reasons why Anglicans are tempted to ignore a document like this. If there *is* a present prospect of unity with Rome, it looks a very distant prospect to many observers today. So why commit scarce resources of time and energy to pursuing it? Perhaps, indeed, the momentum has gone from the whole movement towards Christian unity, as British Churches have turned (with a hint of desperation, at times) either inwards in self-concern or out towards the un-churched world in evangelism. Some ask whether we can afford 'the luxury' of ecumenical work when other priorities press so hard.[14] And if this is felt about ecumenical work in general, how much more so in an area apparently as abstract, 'churchy' and intangible as 'authority in the Church'?

Yet we ignore *The Gift* at our peril: especially those of us who are Anglicans. Unity is a basic requirement if the Church is to believe in itself and to be believable as a sign and instrument of Christ. Unity is an integral part of any true mission to the world. And, for the Anglican Communion, the maintenance of *genuine* communion and the discovery of forms of authority that help us hold that communion, are the very conditions of survival as well as credibility – given the tensions and conflicts which threaten or impair communion among Anglicans both locally and worldwide. We should 'spare no effort to make fast with bonds of peace the unity which the Spirit gives'[15] – and a better understanding and exercise of authority is perhaps the most fundamental of all the 'bonds of peace'. Looking in the mirror that *The Gift* puts before us, we are stimulated to engage more rigorously with the challenges to authenticity in our own Church as well as to engage in closer conversation and partnership with our sister Churches.

Hardened ecumenists know that the kingdom does not come through exertion – even by our most ingenious efforts. Unity in the divided household of faith is 'a gift' in two senses: it is already given to us, in so far as God's Spirit enables us to confess one Lord, one Christ who has already overcome the enmity[16] and alienation which divide human communities; and it will always come to fruition by surprise – as a new event of grace – rather than by entirely planned and predictable moves. At this juncture in the ecumenical movement, it is more clear than ever that the work of conversations, partnerships and strategies for unity has to be seen as laying landing-strips for divine grace: clearings in the jungle of our past (and present) disagreements on which the gift of unity can alight in God's time. That is one reason why praying for unity remains essential to the enterprise.

This collection is offered to encourage *wholehearted*, *intelligent* and *prayerful* engagement with the pursuit of unity among Christians and, particularly, with *The Gift of Authority*.

notes

chapter 1   the context of *The Gift of Authority* in the history of Anglican–Roman Catholic dialogue *(Stephen Platten)*

1   John Robinson, *Honest to God*, SCM Press, 1963.

2   Austen Flannery (ed.), *Vatican Council II: The Conciliar and Post Conciliar Documents*, Costello Publishing, O.P. 1981, 1988, pp. 483ff.

3   Anglican–Roman Catholic International Commission (ARCIC), *The Final Report*, CTS/SPCK, 1982, p. 118.

4   ARCIC, 'The Malta Report' in *The Final Report*, pp. 108ff.

5   ARCIC, 'Eucharistic Doctrine' in *The Final Report*, p. 16, paragraph 12.

6   ARCIC, 'Ministry and Ordination, Co-Chairman's Preface' in *The Final Report*, p. 29.

7   ARCIC, *The Final Report: Authority I*, p. 67, paragraph 26.

8   ARCIC, *The Final Report: Authority I*, p. 64, paragraph 24.

9   ARCIC, *The Final Report: Authority II*, p. 98, paragraph 33.

10 Second Anglican–Roman Catholic International Commission, *The Gift of Authority*: *Authority in the Church III*, CTS/Church House Publishing, 1999, p. 41, paragraph 59.

11 Lambeth Conference, Resolution 8, in Christopher Hill and Edward Yarnold SJ (eds), 1988 *Anglicans and Roman Catholics: The Search for Unity,* SPCK/CTS, 1994, p. 153, paragraph 1.

12 Hill and Yarnold (eds), *Anglicans and Roman Catholics*, p. 153, paragraph 3.

13 'The Official Roman Catholic Response to the Final Report of ARCIC I (1991)' in Hill and Yarnold (eds), *Anglicans and Roman Catholics*, p. 156, paragraph 1.

14 Ibid., p. 156, paragraph 2.

15 ARCIC II, *Clarifications on Eucharist and Ministry*, ACC/PCPCU, 1994.

16 Letter by Cardinal E. Cassidy (President of the Pontifical Council for the Unity of Christians) to the Co-Chairman of ARCIC II (1994) in Hill and Yarnold (eds), *Anglicans and Roman Catholics*, p. 207.

17 *One in Hope*, Common Declaration of Pope John Paul II and the Archbishop of Canterbury (The Most Revd Robert Runcie), CTS/CHP, 1989, p. 21.

18 Pope John Paul II, *Encyclical Letter: Ut Unum Sint*, Libreria Vaticana, 1995, p. 107, paragraphs 95, 96.

19 Second Anglican–Roman Catholic International Commission, *Salvation and the Church*, ACC/Secretariat for Promoting Christian Unity, 1987.

20 'Lambeth Conference 1988' in Hill and Yarnold (eds), *Anglicans and Roman Catholics*, p. 154.

21 Second Anglican–Roman Catholic International Commission, *Church as Communion*, ACC/Pontifical Council for Promoting Christian Unity (CTS) 1991, p. 35, paragraph 57.

22 Second Anglican–Roman Catholic International Commission, *Life in Christ: Morals, Communion and the Church*, ACC/Pontifical Council for Promoting Christian Unity, 1994, p. 33, paragraph 89.

23 ARCIC, *The Final Report*, p. 97, paragraph 32, footnote 7.

24 ARCIC II, *The Gift of Authority*, p. 31, paragraph 42. The text refers to the material in Authority I but uses infallibility directly in its argument about the Church.

25 ARCIC, *The Final Report*, p. 64ff., paragraph 24.

26 ARCIC, *The Final Report*, p. 64ff., paragraph 24(d)

'The claim that the Pope possesses universal immediate jurisdiction, the limits of which are not clearly specified, is a source of anxiety to Anglicans who fear that the way is thus opened to its illegitimate or uncontrolled use. Nevertheless, the First Vatican Council intended that the Papal primacy should be exercised only to maintain and never to erode the structures of the local churches. The Roman Catholic Church is today seeking to replace the juridical outlook of the 19th century by a more pastoral understanding of authority in the church.' This sub-paragraph highlights the dilemma of what precisely is meant by *universal immediate authority* and in which context it may be exercised.

Some further clarity is given in the Methodist/Roman Catholic report on Teaching Authority, *Speaking the Truth in Love* (page 45, paragraph 113): 'He is the "first servant of unity". In order that this ministry may be effective, the jurisdiction of the Bishop of Rome is "universal", "ordinary" and "immediate". His primatial authority is "universal" because it is at the service of the communion of all the churches. It is "ordinary" in that it belongs to him in virtue of his office, rather than as delegated to him by others. It is "immediate" in order to enable him, when necessary for the good of the universal Church, and in faithfulness to the Gospel, to act anywhere in order to preserve the Church's unity in faith and love.' This in itself may oversimplify and for further reference one should be directed to the discussion in the book by Jean Marie Tillard, *The Bishop of Rome* (SPCK 1982). See particularly pages 142–50, the paragraph headed 'The Power of a Bishop among the Bishops'. The crucial passage is that section which runs from page 148 to 150.

27 ARCIC, *The Final Report*, p. 69ff., paragraph 2.

28 ARCIC, *The Final Report*, pp. 97–8, paragraph 33.

chapter 2   authority: gift or threat? *(Mary Tanner)*

1   R.A.K. Runcie, *Authority in Crisis? An Anglican Response*, SCM Press, 1988, p. 22.

2   D.Gill (ed.), *Gathered for Life, Official Report of the VI Assembly of the World Council of Churches*, WCC, 1988, p. 45.

3   *Confessing the One Faith*, Faith and Order Paper 153 (WCC, 1991), *Baptism, Eucharist and Ministry*, Faith and Order Paper 111 (WCC, 1982).

4   *The Gift of Authority: Authority in the Church III, An Agreed Statement by the Second Anglican–Roman Catholic International Commission*, CTS/Church Publishing Incorporated, 1999.

5   *The Final Report of the Anglican–Roman Catholic International Commission*, CTS/SPCK, 1982.

6   C.Hill and E. Yarnold SJ (eds.), *Anglicans and Roman Catholics: The Search for Unity*, SPCK/CTS, 1994, pp. 153–67.

7   *The Truth Shall Make You Free, The Lambeth Conference, 1988*, ACC, 1988, Resolution 18, pp. 216 and 217.

8   *The Virginia Report, The Report of the Inter-Anglican Theological and Doctrinal Commission*, Moorehouse Publishing, 1990.

9   *The Official Report of the Lambeth Conference 1998*, Moorehouse Publishing, 1999, Resolutions III, 6,7 and 8, pp. 396–8.

10 P. C. Rodger and L. Vischer (eds), *The Fourth World Conference on Faith and Order*, Montreal, 1963, Faith and Order Paper 42, SCM Press, 1964, Section II, paragraph 39.

11 *Baptism, Eucharist and Ministry*, World Council of Churches Faith and Order Paper 111, 1982, pp. 25-6 ('Ministry' paragraph 26).

12 *The Final Report*, p. 95

13 *May They All Be One, A Response of the House of Bishops of the Church of England* to Ut Unum Sint, House of Bishops Occasional Paper, Church House Publishing, 1997, p.18.

14 *Towards a Church of England Response to BEM and ARCIC*, Church House Publishing, 1985, p. 97.

15 *The Truth Shall Make You Free*, p. 21.

16 *May They All Be One*, p. 13.

chapter 3 'yes' and 'no' – a response to *The Gift of Authority* (Martin Davie)

1   Second Anglican–Roman Catholic International Commission, *The Gift of Authority*: *Authority in the Church III*, CTS/Church Publishing Incorporated, 1999, p. 13, paragraph 8.

2   Ibid, p.13, paragraph 7.

3   Ibid, p.19, paragraph 19.

4   Ibid, pp. 22–3, paragraphs 26–7.

5   Ibid, p. 23, paragraph 28.

6   Ibid, pp. 21–2, paragraph 25, pp. 34–5, paragraph 48.

7   Ibid, pp. 33–4, paragraph 47.

8   Ibid, p. 42, paragraphs 60–61

9   Ibid, p. 41, paragraphs 58–9

10 See, for example, the recent Meissen and Reuilly agreements with the Lutheran and Reformed Churches in Germany and France where this point is made explicitly, and Canons B 43 and 44 which implicitly recognize the ecclesial reality of non-episcopal Churches and the exercise of *episcope* by their ministers.

11 It is true that a number of major 'non-episcopal' Churches have been discussing episcopacy or introducing forms of episcopacy in recent decades, and it could be argued that this indicates some form of trajectory towards episcopal ministry.

However, this is a case that needs to be argued rather than assumed to be true, and the major problem with *The Gift of Authority* at this point is its failure to acknowledge that the case for episcopacy even needs to be made.

12 Footnote 1 on p.16 of *The Gift of Authority* follows the 1963 Fourth World Conference of Faith and Order in defining Tradition with a capital T as 'the Gospel itself, transmitted from generation to generation in and by the Church.' Clearly if this is what is meant there can be no conflict between tradition and Scripture since Scripture and the Gospel can never be at variance. However, in the discussion of 'Tradition' in the text of *The Gift of Authority*, the way in which the word is used makes it clear that what is being discussed is the process by which the Gospel is transmitted from one generation to the next and the ways in which the Church has sought to give expression to the Gospel in the course of this process.

13 Thomas Cranmer, *A Fruitful Exhortation to the Reading and Knowledge of Holy Scripture* in J. Leith (ed.), *Creeds of the Churches*, revised edn, Basil Blackwell, 1973, p. 232.

14 *The Gift of Authority*, p. 22, paragraph 25.

15 Text in C. Hill and E. Yarnold SJ (eds), *Anglicans and Roman Catholics: The Search for Unity*, SPCK/CTS, 1994 p. 56. It could be objected that this way of formulating the matter leaves no space for what came to be known at the Reformation as *adiaphora*, that is to say, practices that are retained or allowed in the Church although they are not commanded by Scripture itself. This objection fails to note, however, that those such as Richard Hooker who argued for the retention of *adiaphora* did so because they believed that the practices concerned, although not explicitly commanded by Scripture, were consonant with that overall pattern of Christian practice which could be found in Scripture.

16 *The Gift of Authority,* p. 30, paragraph 41.

17 Ibid, p. 30, paragraph 42.

18 It could be argued that the practice of mono episcopacy is an example of a tradition which stems from the apostles but is not contained in Scripture, but this is a disputed point and would need to be defended against those who would argue that mono episcopacy emerged in the second-century Church without apostolic sanction.

19 See for example Articles XIX and XXI of the *Thirty-Nine Articles* which maintain that both local churches and General Councils of the Church are susceptible to error.

20 See St Augustine, *The City of God*, XVIII: 49: 'many reprobates are mingled in the Church with the good, and both sorts are collected as it were in the dragnet of the gospel; and in this world, as in a sea swim without separation, enclosed in nets until the shore is reached.'

21 *The Gift of Authority*, p. 15, paragraph 12.

22 Ibid., p. 15, paragraph 12.

23 K. Barth, *Evangelical Theology*, Fontana, 1969, pp. 44–5.

24 *The Gift of Authority*, p. 27, paragraph 36.

25 See the questions addressed to the candidate for episcopal ordination in the BCP ordinal and the declaration and questions in the ASB ordinal and the duties of the bishop laid down in Canon C 18.

26 *The Gift of Authority* p. 28, paragraph 38.

27 Ibid, p. 29, paragraph 39.

28 Letter from Ronald B. Young in *Episcopal Life*, July/August 1999.

29 *The Gift of Authority*, p. 32, paragraph 44.

30 Ibid, pp. 30–31, paragraph 42.

31 Ibid, p. 31, paragraph 43.

32 Ibid., footnote 2, p. 31.

33 *Doctrine in the Church of England*, SPCK, 1938, p. 36.

34 W. H. Griffith Thomas, *The Catholic Faith*, Church Book Room Press, second revised edn, 1952, p. 214.

35 Ibid, p. 214.

36 *The Gift of Authority*, p. 35, paragraph 49.

37 Ibid, p. 32, paragraph 44.

38 *The Porvoo Common Statement*, CCU, 1993, p. 23.

39 Ibid, p. 26.

40 *The Gift of Authority*, p. 32, paragraph 44.

41 *May They All Be One, A Response of the House of Bishops of the Church of England to* Ut Unum Sint, House of Bishops Occasional Paper, Church House Publishing, 1997, p. 17.

42 *The Gift of Authority*, p. 32, paragraph 46.

43 Ibid, p. 33, paragraph 46.

44 *Authority in the Church II*: 7 in Hill and Yarnold (eds), Anglicans and Roman Catholics, p. 64.

45 *First Dogmatic Constitution on the Church of Christ*, Chs I & II in Leith (ed.), *Creeds of the Churches*, pp. 449 and 451.

46 *The Gift of Authority*, p. 34, paragraph 47.

47 It needs to be noted also that the previous ARCIC report, Authority in the Church II, specifically noted that: 'neither general councils nor universal primates are invariably preserved from error even in official declarations' (*Authority in the Church II*, paragraph 27, in Hill and Yarnold (eds), *Anglicans and Roman Catholics*, p. 72).

48 This is a point that is strongly made by Bishop Colin Buchanan in the *Church of England Newspaper* on 30 July 1999. Bishop Michael Nazir-Ali, who was a member of the Commission, has criticized Bishop Buchanan's argument, but Bishop Buchanan's interpretation does seem to represent the most straightforward reading of the text itself.

49 *The Gift of Authority*, p. 35, paragraph 48.

50 Church of England Faith and Order Advisory Group on *The Final Report of ARCIC I* (1985) in Hill and Yarnold (eds), *Anglicans and Roman Catholics*, p. 148.

51 *May They All Be One*, pp. 17–18

52 *The Gift of Authority*, p. 42, paragraph 60.

chapter 4   an ecumenical hermeneutic of trust
(Christopher Hill)

1   For a fuller presentation of the background to *The Gift of Authority* see Stephen
    Platten's introductory essay, chapter 1.

2   *The Emmaus Report: A report of the Anglican Ecumenical Consultation which took
    place at The Emmaus Retreat Centre, West Wickham, Kent, England 27 January–2
    February 1987 in preparation for ACC-7, Singapore, 1987 and The Lambeth Conference
    1988*, Church House Publishing, 1987.

3   *The Gift of Authority*, p. 11, paragraph 1.

4   ARCIC I was accused of a similar reticence of language. Churches of the Reformation
    (including our own) have used much bolder language – 'Councils may err'. Here we
    have to understand that we are talking about a *joint* text, which also necessarily
    reflects something of the culture of the contemporary RC tradition. Rome is currently
    oversensitive to criticism. Its critics use coded diplomatic language. The recent book
    by the former Archbishop of San Francisco, James Quinn, *The Reform of the Papacy:
    the costly call to Christian unity* is a case in point. In a *Tablet* review (11 December
    1999), Nicholas Lash said: 'Quinn's book had it been published in say 1965 would
    probably have caused little comment. It now seems courageous, even radical.' Yet it
    conforms to the gently coded irenic language of Roman Catholic reformers, so that it
    may be heard by those who need to hear it. Anglicans may regret the gentle language
    of *The Gift of Authority*. But we must not thereby fail to hear the radical practical
    questions of authority it raises for the contemporary Roman Catholic Church.

5   We owe this acute observation of Anglican Synodical procedure owing more to
    parliamentary practice than true synodality to the former Co-Chairman of ARCIC II,
    Bishop Mark Santer.

6   Herder and Herder, 1999.

7   The French Catholic Church continued to maintain many emphases of the Medieval
    conciliar reform movement. Such emphases and structures were also inherited by the
    reformed Church of England, leading to significant Anglo-French conversations in the
    early seventeenth century. The 'Gallicans' maintained that a majority of bishops in
    council could annul a decision by the Pope, or at least that the Pope required the
    agreement of the majority of the episcopate. Vatican I rejected this, in a famous
    phrase, affirming that the Pope could teach definitively on his own authority 'and
    not by the consent of the church' (*non autem ex consensu ecclesiae*).

chapter 5   *The Gift of Authority* in the Church of England: sketching a contextual theology *(Martyn Percy)*

1   An earlier version of this paper appears in my *Salt of the Earth: Religious Resilience
    in a Secular Age*, Sheffield Academic Press, 2001.

2   N. Healy, *Church, World and the Christian Life: Practical–Prophetic Ecclesiology*,
    Cambridge University Press, 2000, p. 3 and p. 185; italics mine throughout.

3   E. Farley, *The Fragility of Knowledge: Theological Education in the Church and
    University*, Fortress Press, 1988, p. 180.

4   N. Healy, *Church, World and the Christian Life*.

5   Ibid., p. 26.

6   A. Dulles, *Models of the Church*, Doubleday, 1974/1987.

7   N. Healy, *Church, World and the Christian Life*, p. 34.

8   Ibid., p. 36.

9   Ibid., p. 39.

10 On this, see my essay in M. Percy and A. Walker (eds), *Restoring the Image: Essays in Honour of David Martin*, Sheffield Academic Press, 2001.

11 N. Healy, *Church, World and the Christian Life*, p. 50.

12 Ibid., p. 54.

13 Ironically, the word 'blueprint' does not appear in the *Oxford English Dictionary*; its etymology lies with the German term Blauplan, meaning 'fundamental plan' – but it is clear that such plans are of human design and not divine origin. Cf. R. Dawkins, *River Out of Eden*, Weidenfeld & Nicholson, 1995.

14 I owe a particular debt of gratitude to Dr Ralph Norman, Stephenson Fellow at the University of Sheffield, for his conversation and thoughts in this section, to members of the Archbishops' Faith and Order Advisory Group, and numerous shorter articles that have appeared on the subject, including Joseph Cassidy's commentary in *Affirming Catholicism*, vol. 1, no.1, Autumn 2001, pp. 4–5.

15 *The Gift of Authority*, p. 39, paragraph 52.

16 Ralph Norman, *Notes on ARCIC III* (unpublished paper), 1999, pp. 1–3.

17 *The Gift of Authority*, p. 16, paragraph 14, footnote 1.

18 *The Gift of Authority*, pp. 14, 17, 20–26.

19 *The Gift of Authority*, p. 18, paragraph 18.

20 Norman, *Notes*, p. 4. Witness the argument from silence in paragraph 24.

21 S. Platten, *Augustine's Legacy: Authority and Leadership in the Anglican Communion*, Darton Longman and Todd, 1997.

22 See P. Berger, *The Heretical Imperative*, Collins, 1984, for a fuller discussion of the inductive theological strategy.

23 P. Avis, *Ecumenical Theology and the Elusiveness of Doctrine*, SPCK, 1986, p. x–xii.

24 P. Avis, *Ecumenical Theology*, p. 77.

25 R. Norman, *Notes*, pp. 3–5.

26 *The Gift of Authority*, p. 24, paragraph 30.

27 *The Gift of Authority*, p. 42. Cf. R. Norman, *Notes*, pp. 4–5.

28 *The Gift of Authority*, pp. 45–7.

29 Cf. Lindbeck, *The Nature of Doctrine*, Westminster Press, 1983, p. 16.

30 J. Macquarrie, 'Structures for Unity' in M. Santer (ed.), *Their Lord and Ours: Approaches to Authority, Community and the Unity of the Church*, SPCK, 1982, p. 119.

31 R. Norman, *Notes*, p. 4.

32 Although we should note that the petition to be delivered from 'the tyranny of Rome and all his detestable enormities', included in the Litany of the 1549 Prayer Book,

did not survive the Elizabethan Settlement. Equally, it is clear that the Pope does have some jurisdiction in England, and that *Article xxxvii* should not be read literally.

33 D. Gomez and M. Sinclair, *To Mend the Net: Anglican Faith and Order for Renewed Mission*, The Ekklesia Society, 2001.

34 Ibid., p. 9.

35 Ibid., p. 21.

36 See the discussion of *The Virginia Report* (1995) in Gomez and Sinclair, *To Mend the Net*, p. 11.

37 See N. Sagovsky, *Christian Origins and the Practice of Ecumenism*, Cambridge University Press, 2000.

38 See M. Kennedy, 'A Paper for the Armagh Clerical Union', September 1999.

39 Although this may be no more than a form of subsidiarity that preserves hegemony; ultramontanism welded to managerial culture in the name of modernization.

40 See N. Doe, *The Legal Framework of the Church of England*, Clarendon Press, 1996, chapter 3. Cf. S. Sykes, 'Power in the Church of England', *Concilium*, no. 197, April 1988, pp. 123ff.

41 Cultural differences in Roman Catholicism should again be noted. Anglican priests from the Diocese of Lincoln (including women) have been known to con-celebrate the Eucharist, for example, with a Roman Catholic bishop at his cathedral in Belgium. In England, those same Anglican priests would normally be excluded from even receiving at a Mass.

42 G. Neville, *Radical Churchman: Edward Lee Hicks and the New Liberalism*, Clarendon Press, 1998, p. 14.

43 N. Healy, *Church, World and the Christian Life*, p. 155.

44 For further discussion see M. Percy, 'Label or Libel' in L. Francis (ed.), *Sociology, Theology and the Curriculum*, Cassell, 1999, pp. 82–92.

45 N. Healy, *Church, World and the Christian Life,* p. 185.

46 D. Tracy, *The Analogical Imagination*, SCM Press, pp. ix, 393.

47 N. Healy, *Church, World and the Christian Life*, p. 3.

48 For further discussion see D. Tracy, 'Defending the Public Character of Theology' in J. Wall (ed.), *Theologians in Transition*, Crossroad, 1981, pp. 116ff.

49 P. Lakeland, *Postmodernity: Christian Identity in a Fragmented Age*, Fortress Press, 1997, p. 88.

50 K. Tanner, *Theories of Culture: A New Agenda for Theology*, Fortress Press, 1997, pp. 87–92.

51 Z. Sardar and B. Van Loon, *Introducing Cultural Studies*, Icon Books, 1999, p. 9.

52 Cf. Don S. Browning, *Fundamental Practical Theology*, Fortress Press, 2000, pp. 1–9.

53 *The Shorter Oxford English Dictionary on Historical Principles*, Oxford University Press, 1978, p. 134.

chapter 6   it's the thought that counts: reflections from local contexts in England *(Flora Winfield)*

1   For a more detailed consideration of the ecclesial nature of these ecumenical structures, see my article 'Seen and Unseen: Explicit and Implicit Ecclesiology in a Local Ecumenical Partnership' in Colin Podmore (ed.), *Community, Unity, Communion: Essays in Honour of Mary Tanner*, Church House Publishing, 1998.

chapter 7   in conclusion   *(Peter Fisher)*

1   See, for example, Jesus' repeated questions about the Hebrew Scriptures: 'What is written in the Law? . . . What do you read there?' (Luke 10.26), 'What did Moses command you?', 'Does not scripture say . . .?' (Mark 10.3; 11.17), etc.

2   See particularly the essays by Christopher Hill and Mary Tanner.

3   Though not synonymous with 'Roman Catholic' and 'Anglican', these two terms evoke something of the culture of mistrust that has helped to maintain division – and even hostility – between the two traditions since the Reformation.

4   See particularly the essays by Martin Davie and Martyn Percy.

5   Quoted in *The Tablet*, 15 May 1999, p. 680.

6   Onora O'Neill, Reith Lecture I, page 2, cited from www.bbc.co.uk/radio4/reith2002.

7   The most frequent meaning of the Greek word *oikoumene*, from which our word 'ecumenical' derives, is 'the whole inhabited earth'.

8   R. R. Ruether, *Women–Church, Theology and Practice of Liturgical Communities*, Harper and Row, 1985, pp. 57–8.

9   Letty M. Russell, *Household of Freedom, Authority in Feminist Theology*, Westminster Press, 1987, p. 34.

10 Ibid., p. 63.

11 Ibid., p. 58.

12 The Ven. Dr Joy Tetley, in an unpublished paper 'The Use of the Bible in Ecumenical Dialogue Involving Anglicans' (prepared for the Faith and Order Advisory Group), p. 18. Dr Tetley also makes more general observations about the understanding of Scripture in these dialogues.

13 From the same unpublished paper, page 20, paragraph 4.2.

14 Notably, when the Archbishops' Council of the Church of England proposed a set of priorities for the national Church's work (to the General Synod, in 2001), ecumenical endeavour was only added to the list as a result of strong representations by Synod members.

15 Ephesians 4.3.

16 Ephesians 2.14.

index

adiaphora 112 n.15
'Amen' to God's 'Yes' 13, 18–19, 21, 22, 30, 33–4, 40, 41–2, 63–5, 72–3, 95
Anglican Centre (Rome) 4
Anglican Consultative Council 6, 17, 61
Anglicanism
  challenges to 28–9, 31
  and contextual theology 76–93
  and diversity 82–3, 85–6
  and ecclesiology 82–4, 85
  Evangelical viii, 20, 33–59
  and exercise of authority viii, 16–18, 23, 31, 62–3, 76–93
  and experience of living in dialogue 96–7
  and grass-roots support 87, 93
  and nature of communion 17, 63, 80, 82–3, 107
  and primacy 17, 26, 36
  and provincial autonomy 10, 16–17, 63, 68–9, 85
  response to *The Gift of Authority* 6–7
  and synodical government 46–7, 62, 67–9, 87
Anglo-catholicism, 'romantic' 65
Apostolicae Curae
  of Leo XIII 56, 88
  of Pius XI 87–8
apostolicity 70
  and episcopal ministry 50–51, 57
Archbishops' Council (CofE) 86, 117 n.15
ARCIC I 4–5
  Authority in the Church I (1977) 5, 6, 39, 40, 52–4, 56, 60–62
  Authority in the Church II 5–6, 11, 25, 40, 52–4, 56, 60–62, 112 n.47
  Elucidation (1981) 5, 6, 11, 39, 60–61
  Final Report 6, 7, 15
  methodology viii, 5, 8, 9, 10, 62
  responses to 6–9, 29, 54
  and reticence of language 114 n.4a
  Statement on the Eucharist (1971) 5, 7
  Statement on Ministry and Ordination (1973) 75
ARCIC II
  Church as Communion 9–10
  Clarifications (1993) 7, 8
  Life in Christ: Morals, Communion and the Church 10

Salvation and the Church 9
  see also *The Gift of Authority*
Arianism 39, 41, 66
Assisi meetings 26, 29, 31–2
Augustine of Hippo, St 41
authenticity, and authority 18, 51–2, 77, 92
authority
  and authenticity 18, 51–2, 77, 92
  of Christ 80
  in the Church 18–22, 63–73
  in contemporary culture 2–3, 12–13, 62, 73, 75, 95, 102–3
  and contextual theology 76–93
  dispersed 11, 85, 88
  as domination 104
  episcopal 43–4, 84
  as evangelical 35
  exercise of 16–18, 21, 22–6, 31, 35–6, 63–73, 75, 76–95, 95
  as gift 16, 19, 21–2, 30–31, 62, 74, 87, 102
  misuse of 63–4
  obedience to 43, 57, 66, 87–8, 92
  and ordination of women 8–9
  as partnership 106
  as personal, relational and integral to faith 63–4
  and power viii, 14, 63, 87–8, 102, 103
  of Scripture 20, 35, 39, 52, 65–6, 72–3
  teaching 44–52, 64, 69
  of Tradition 37–9, 40, 72–3, 81
Avis, Paul 83

baptism, and community 19
Baptism, Eucharist and Ministry 22–3, 61, 96
Barth, Karl 42–3, 77
Bea, Card. Augustin 1
Bell, George 2
BEM see *Baptism, Eucharist and Ministry*
bishops
  and apostolicity 50–51, 57
  and episcopal authority 43–4
  and infallibility 23–5, 70, 84
  and local church 22, 56, 68, 103
  oversight in 62
  as subject to reformation 36, 73
  and synodality 46–7, 62, 68–9

and teaching authority 23–4, 44–52, 64, 80
  see also collegiality; oversight
Book of Common Prayer 63, 113–14 n.32
Buchanan, Colin 16, 112 n.48
Bultmann, Rudolf 3

Called to Be One 96
Canon Law, Anglican
  Ecumenical Canons viii, 37, 110 n.10b
  and teaching authority of bishops 45–6
Canon Law, Roman, and obedience to
  bishop 44
Canterbury, Archbishop of
and Anglican Communion 17, 26, 68–9, 82,
  85
as primate 26, 74
Carey, George, Archbishop of Canterbury
  29–30, 31–2, 61
Cassidy, Card. E. 7
Cassidy, Joseph 115 n.14
catholicity 7, 21, 54, 66
Chadwick, Henry 16
Church
  and apostolicity 50–51
  as communion see koinonia
  and development 20, 22
  and diversity 15, 20–22, 28, 30, 36,
    39, 66, 82–3, 95, 99
  and exercise of authority 16–18, 21,
    22–6, 31, 63–73, 76–93, 95
  and indefectibility 24, 26, 40–41, 42,
    66, 70–71, 80, 84, 87
  and infallibility 11, 23–6, 27, 48,
    70–71, 80
  and magisterium 23, 69, 83, 84, 102
  models of 19, 22, 30, 77–9
  and non-episcopal Churches 37, 110
    nn.10b,11b
  and place of authority 18–22
  see also error
Church of England
  and catholicity 86–7
  and contextual theology 79–93
  and establishment 86–7
  and laity 86–7
  orders 56, 88, 93
  see also Anglicanism; Thirty-Nine Articles
church, local 21, 37
  and bishop of Rome 16, 28, 53, 56, 72
  and bishops 22, 56, 68, 103
  and collegiality 30–31
  and ecumenism 94–90
  and individual faith 19, 81
  and papal jurisdiction 56–7, 73–4
  and synodality 67–8

clergy
  and laity 67
  and synodality 47, 62
  and teaching authority 44–5, 48, 64
Coggan, Donald, Archbishop of Canterbury 5
college of bishops see collegiality
collegiality 22–5, 26–7, 34, 74
  and apostolicity 50–51, 57, 70
  and infallibility 84
  as instrument of unity 6
  and jurisdiction 57
  and primacy 6, 26, 28, 30, 36, 60–62,
    72, 80
  and teaching authority 47–8
  and unanimity 51–2
common life 97
conciliarity 6, 11, 60–61, 67, 70–72
  and reception 71–2
Congar, Yves 5
Congregation of the Doctrine of the Faith,
  Observations 7
conscience, individual 24, 42–3, 49–50,
  59, 64–5, 73
consent
  in Church of England 86–7
  universal 48–9, 59
Couturier, Abbé Paul 2
Cranmer, Thomas 38
creation, purpose of God 18–19, 21, 33
culture
  and attitudes to authority 2–3, 12–13,
    62, 73–5, 95, 102–3
  and ecclesiology viii, 76, 79, 85–93, 94
Curia, Roman 1, 28, 69, 73–4

Davie, Martin 33–59, 101
death of God theology 3
dialogue see ecumenism
discernment 34
  and Bishop of Rome 27, 63
  by the whole Church 23–6, 35–6, 44, 67
dissent, right to 24, 44, 59, 73
diversity 15, 20–22, 28, 30, 36, 39, 95, 99
  in Anglicanism 82–3, 85–6
  and catholicity 21, 66–7
  of ministry 37
  in Roman Catholicism 17
  'divine right' 11
doctrine
  in Anglicanism 83
  consent to 27, 49–50, 59, 71–2
Doctrine in the Church of England (1938)
  49–50
Dogmatic Constitution of the Church of Christ
  54, 57

domination, authority as 104
Dulles, A. 77–8

ecclesiology
 Anglican 82–8
 'blueprint' 18, 77–9, 88, 92–3
 concrete 77, 78–9, 81, 88, 92–3
 episodic 70
 'practical-prophetic' 76, 77, 79, 89–92
 Roman Catholic 71, 84
ecumenism
 and ad limina visits 6, 28, 69–70
 and apostolicity 50–51
 early history 1–4
 and ecumenical methodology viii, 5, 8,
  9, 10, 62, 67, 76–7
 grass-roots 77, 86, 93, 94–9, 102, 103
 as lived dialogue 96–7
 and non-episcopal Churches 37
 and other partners 15, 95
 and Scripture 20, 106
 and Tradition 20
 and visible unity 14–15
 see also ARCIC
Edinburgh Conference (1910) 2
Emmaus Report (1987) 6, 61
empiricism, and ecclesiology 83
episcopacy
 and ministry of memory 21, 22, 24, 30,
  40, 67, 70, 84
 mono-episcopacy 37, 111 n.18
 and Tradition 84
Episcopal Conferences (RC) 7, 8, 17, 69, 74
error
 in the Church 40–41, 42, 49, 86
 and ecumenical councils 55, 71
 and papacy 55–6, 69
 preservation from 11, 23, 48, 59, 70, 84
 and transmission of Tradition 38, 66
Eucharist, and lay presidency 16
Evangelicalism, and response to Gift of
 Authority viii, 33–59
existentialism 2, 12

faith, of individual and community 21,
 41–3, 64–6
Faith and Order Advisory Group vii, 56, 114
 n.14
Faith and Order Conference 1963 20, III n.12
faith and order movement 2
Farley, Edward 76
feminist theology 104–5
First Vatican Council 11, 54–5, 71, 73–4,
 109 n.26, 113 n.7
Fisher, Geoffrey, Archbishop of Canterbury
 1–2, 12

Fisher, Peter 100–107

Gallicanism 74, 113 n.7a
General Councils 55, 67, 70–72
General Synod, role 8–9, 46, 68, 86
The Gift of Authority
 and basis in Scripture 18, 33, 64, 105
 and catholicity 54, 66
 challenges to each Communion 28–9, 31
 and conciliarity 70–72
 context 1–13
 and ecumenical methodology viii, 62, 67
 and exercise of authority 16–18, 22–6,
  31–2, 67
 and grass-roots ecumenism 77, 86,
  93, 94–9, 102, 103
 helpful aspects 35–7, 92
 and misuse of authority 63
 problem areas 34–5, 37–58, 59, 86–8,
  101
 responses to vii–viii, 13, 16, 32, 60,
  100–7
 and reticence of language 57, 66, 70, 73
 and steps to visible unity 73–5, 107
 see also 'Amen' to God's 'Yes'; collegiality;
  idealization of the Church;
  indefectibility; infallibility; primacy;
  Scripture; sin and weakness; synodality;
  Tradition
Gomez, Drexel and Sinclair, Maurice 84–6
grace see authority, as gift
Griffith Thomas, W. H. 50

Hampton, Stephen 16
Healy, Nicholas 76, 77–9, 89, 92
hermeneutic
 of suspicion 101
 of trust 60–75, 100
hierarchy, structural 15, 18, 22, 30, 57,
 64, 87, 102, 105
Hill, Christopher 60–75, 101
Hinsley, Card. Arthur 2
Holy Spirit
 as active in the Church 61, 64, 66,
  71–3, 81, 84
 and canon of Scripture 66
 and contemporary culture 89–90
 and ecumenical dialogue 97–8
 and indefectibility of the Church 25–6,
  40, 66, 70–71, 84
 and individual conscience 50
 and ministry of oversight 48, 51
 and prophecy 45
 and Tradition 23, 35–6, 40, 65
 and unity 107
homosexuality 16, 86

Hooker, Richard 83, 111 n.15
House of Bishops
  and authoritative teaching 69
  and doctrine 46
  and primacy 27, 32, 53
humanity, and response to God 18–19,
    21, 22, 30, 33–4, 64, 72

idealization of the Church viii, 21, 81, 84,
    85, 101
  and blueprint ecclesiologies 18, 77–9,
    88, 92–3
  and grassroots ecumenism 95
Ind, Bill, Bishop of Truro 15
indefectibility 24, 26, 40–41, 42, 66,
    70–71, 80, 84, 87
individualism
  postmodern 3, 73
  Protestant 64–5
infallibility 29, 61, 66
  of the Church's teaching 11, 23–6, 27,
    48, 70–73, 80
  and collegiality 84
  and human weakness 25, 55
  papal 27, 61, 73, 80
  and reception by the whole Church 27, 30
Inter-Anglican Theological and Doctrinal
    Commission 17
International Anglican-Roman Catholic
    Commission on Unity and Mission 31

Jewel, John 49
John XXIII, Pope 1–2, 12
John Paul II, Pope 7, 8, 17, 29–30, 31–2
  Ut Unum Sint vii, 9, 27, 32, 55–6, 63
jurisdiction
  immediate 11, 58, 59, 61, 110 n.26
  and local church 56–7, 73–4

kenosis, and dialogue 98
Kierkegaard, Sören 3
koinonia 5, 6, 9–10, 15
  and Anglicanism 17, 80, 83, 85
  and oversight 22
  and provincial autonomy 28, 68–9
  and synodality 68
Küng, Hans 16, 71

laity
  in Church of England 86–7, 93
  and exercise of authority 23, 61, 63,
    65, 67, 85
  and hierarchy 15
  role 10, 11, 17, 22
  in Roman Catholic Church 28, 36, 47, 63

and synodality 23, 31, 46–7, 62
and teaching authority 44–5, 48, 64
Lakeland, Paul 90
Lambeth Conference
  1988 6, 8, 9, 16, 31, 52, 60–62, 74
  1998 17, 68–9, 75
    Resolution on Human Sexuality 87
Lash, Nicholas 113 n.4a
lay presidency 16
Leo XIII, Pope, Apostolicae Curae 56, 87
liberalism, individualistic 65
liberation theology 104
life and work movement 2
Lima document see Baptism, Eucharist and
    Ministry
Lindbeck, George A. 90
Longley, Clifford 16
Lubac, Henri de 5
Lumen Gentium 48, 57
Luther, Martin 44, 45

Macquarrie, John 3, 84, 114 n.30
magisterium 23, 69, 83, 84, 102
Malta Report (1968) 4
May They All Be One vii, 52, 56–7
memory, corporate 65, 66, 81, 84
Milbank, John 90
ministry
  diversity of forms 37
  of memory 21, 22, 24, 30, 40, 67, 70, 84
  as personal and collegial 23
  threefold order 86
  see also oversight
mission
  and exercise of authority 28, 66, 67,
    68–9, 75
  and unity 98, 106
Montefiore, Hugh 70
mutuality 93, 96

Nazir-Ali, Michael 112 n.48
Neville, Graham 88
Niagara Report 66
Nicaea, Council (325) 66, 71
Norman, Ralph 80–81, 83–4, 114 n.14

obedience, and authority 43, 57, 66, 87–8,
    92
O'Neill, Onora 102–3
orders, Anglican 56, 88, 93
Ordinals
  and canonical obedience 44
  and teaching authority of bishops 45–6
ordination
  of practising homosexuals 16, 86

of women 8–9, 16–17, 86
Orthodox Churches 39, 74
oversight, ministry of
and acceptance of episcopal authority
43–4
and Anglican Communion 28
and apostolicity 50–51, 70
and exercise of authority 67–73
and koinonia 22
in non-episcopal Churches 37, 110–11 n.11b
and primacy 84
and Roman Curia 28, 69, 73–4
shared 28
see also bishops

papacy
and immediate jurisdiction 11, 56–7,
58, 59, 61, 73–4, 109 n.26
and reform 55–6, 73–4
and ultramontanism 69
see also primacy; Rome, Bishop of
paradosis see Tradition
participation, active 97
partnership, authority as 104–5
patriarchy, in the Church 104
Paul VI, Pope 4, 5
Percy, Martyn 76–94, 101
Pius XI, Pope, Apostolicae Curae 87–8
Platten, Stephen 1–13, 82, 101
Pontifical Council for Promoting Christian
Unity 2, 7
Porvoo Common Statement 50–51
postmodernism vii, 12, 14, 62, 73, 75
power, and authority viii, 14, 63, 87–8, 102,
103
priesthood see ordination
primacy
in Anglicanism 17, 26, 36
and collegiality 26, 28, 30, 36, 60–62,
72, 80
and conciliarity 6, 11, 60, 61
and episcopacy 84
as gift 26
as instrument of unity 6, 11, 26, 29,
32, 60, 62–3, 69, 73, 85
papal 26–7, 31–2, 52–7, 80
Petrine 4, 8, 53–5
as 'presiding in love' 8
provisional recognition of viii, 29, 58, 73–4
re-reception of 28–9, 31–2, 58
and Scripture and Tradition 60, 72
and ultramontanism 69
universal vii, 6, 9–10, 11, 52, 62, 72,
73–4, 80
Primates' Meeting 17, 85

prophecy, as authoritative 45
provinces, Anglican 10, 16–17, 28, 63, 85
and primacy 61

Quinn, James 74, 113 n.4a

Rahner, Karl 77
Ramsey, Michael 4
Ratzinger, Card. Joseph 69
reception
critical 64–5
of episcopal teaching 24–6, 27,
47–50, 71–3, 74–5
and infallibility 27, 30
and primacy 28–9, 31–2, 58
and re-reception 28–9, 31–2, 66
and Tradition 19–21, 30, 34, 65–6,
81, 97–8
redemption, and purpose of God 18–19, 21,
33
Reformation
and ecclesiology 70
and Tradition 20, 36, 38, 39
Robinson, John, Honest to God 3
Roman Catholicism
challenges to 28–9, 31
and the Church 4
and diversity 17
and ecclesiology 71, 84
and Episcopal Conferences 7, 8, 17, 69, 74
and exercise of authority viii, 16–18,
23, 31, 35–6, 62, 63–4, 67, 69
and experience of living in dialogue 96–7
and laity 28, 36, 47, 63
response to The Gift of Authority 7–9
and role of laity 28, 47, 63
and synodical structures 17, 47, 80
see also First Vatican Council; Second
Vatican Council
Rome, Bishop of
and infallibility 27, 61, 73
and local churches 16, 28, 53, 56–7,
72, 74
and primacy 10, 26–7, 31–2, 53–5,
62, 72, 80
re-reception of 28–9, 31–2
as symbol of unity 29, 32, 60, 62–3
see also collegiality
Ruether, Rosemary Radford 104
Runcie, Robert, Archbishop of Canterbury 7,
8, 14, 31–2
Russell, Letty M. 104–5

Salvation and the Church 9
Santer, Mark 103, 113 n.5

Sardar, Z. and Van Loon, B. 91, 115 n.51
Sartre, Jean-Paul 3
Scripture
    authority of 20, 35, 39, 52, 65–6, 72–3
    and conciliarity 71
    in ecumenical dialogue 105–6
    and infallibility 30, 48
    and primacy 60, 72–3
    and Tradition 20–22, 35, 37–9, 48,
        65, 73, 81
    Second Vatican Council 1–2, 4, 5, 17, 28,
        48, 69, 74
sensus fidei 21, 43, 48, 67, 72, 83
sensus fidelium 21, 24–5, 34, 49, 59, 61,
    67, 84
sin and weakness
    and authority structures 30, 63–4
    and infallibility 25, 55
    and Tradition 19–20, 34, 36, 38, 41,
        66, 81
situation ethics 3
social science, and ecclesiology 88
'South Bank theology' 3
Speaking the Truth in Love 109 n.26
subsidiarity 80, 82, 115 n.39
succession, apostolic 51, 70, 86, 88
'Sword of the Spirit' movement 2
Synod of Bishops (RC) 17, 69, 74
synodality 22–3, 28, 30–31, 46–7,
    67–9, 74–5, 80
    eucharistic and parliamentary models
        47, 68, 69, 114 n.5a

Tanner, Kathryn 90–92
Tanner, Mary 14–32, 101
teaching
    authoritative 30, 44–52, 64, 69, 80
    and magisterium 23, 69, 83, 84, 102
    and reception 24–6, 27, 47–50, 71–3
    and unanimity of episcopal college 51–2
Tetley, Joy 105–6
theology
    contextual 76–93
    and faith of the community 42–3
    feminist 104
    interrogative 91
    liberation 104
    and primacy 28–9, 87
Thirty-Nine Articles 41, 55, 62, 70–71,
    84, 111 n.19
Tillard, Jean-Marie 5, 77, 109 n.26
Tillich, Paul 3
Tompkins, Oliver 2
Tracy, David 90
Tradition
    authority of 37–9, 40, 72–3, 81

as borne by whole Church 21, 66–7, 81
as complete 84
and conciliarity 71
and the Holy Spirit 23, 35–6, 40, 65
    and human sin 19–20, 34, 36, 38,
        41, 66, 81
as indefectible 84
and infallibility 30, 48
as paradosis 65
and primacy 60, 72–3
reception and re-reception 19–21, 30, 34,
    65–6, 81, 97–8
and role of bishops 23, 36, 70
and Scripture 20–22, 35, 37–9, 48,
    65, 73, 81
and theology 42–3
and uniformity and diversity 38–9
truth
    'personalist' view 83
    and reception 24, 71–2
    and Tradition 81
    and unanimity 48–9, 52, 59, 84
    as work of the Holy Spirit 23, 25–6,
        40, 65, 66, 70

ultramontanism 69, 115 n.39
unanimity, and truth 48–9, 52, 59, 84
Unitatis Redintegratio 4
unity, visible viii, 14–15, 29–30, 31, 73–5,
    96, 107
    and compromise 101
    as gift 107
    and mission 99, 107
    primacy as instrument of 6, 11, 26,
        29, 32, 60, 62–3, 69, 85
Ut Unum Sint vii, 9, 27, 32, 55–6, 63

Vatican
    Secretariat for the Promotion of Unity 1, 6
    Secretariat of State 1
The Virginia Report 17, 63, 68, 115 n.36
visions, and teaching authority 45
visits, ad limina 6, 28, 69–70

Wainwright, Geoffrey 69
Week of Prayer for Christian Unity 2
Winfield, Flora 102, 104
Wittgenstein, Ludwig 3
women, ordination to priesthood 8–9,
    16–17, 86
World Council of Churches 2, 15
    Faith and Order Commission see
        Baptism, Eucharist and Ministry

Young, Ronald 46